ALL THE WAY HOME

ALL THE WAY HOME

Keith J. Karren

Bookcraft
Salt Lake City, Utah

Copyright © 1986 by Bookcraft, Inc.

All rights reserved. This book or any part thereof may not be reproduced in any form whatsoever, whether by graphic, visual, electronic, filming, microfilming, tape recording, or any other means, without the prior written permission of Bookcraft, Inc., except in the case of brief passages embodied in critical reviews and articles.

Library of Congress Catalog Card Number: 85-73842
ISBN 0-88494-586-3

First Printing, 1986

Printed in the United States of America

*To all whose lives were lost or forever touched
by the war in Vietnam*

TABLE OF CONTENTS

Acknowledgments ix

Prologue 1

Vietnam

1	Toward a Different Education	5
2	"The Few, the Proud . . ."	12
3	Hotel Company	35
4	Point Man	55
5	Wheels	76

Utah

6	The Taste of Failure	93
7	Jan	102
8	Back on the Track	114
9	Garnering the Gold	129
10	The Big Year	139
11	"The Dumbest Thing!"	147
12	New Loves, New Lessons	150
13	A Different Treasure	164
14	Home	177

ACKNOWLEDGMENTS

I wish to thank Sharon Christenson and Lavina Fielding Anderson for their writing and editing help, and Joyce Peterson for the many hours of typing she spent on the manuscript.

I express my deepest appreciation to Diane, my wife, and our children; and to Mike's wife, Jan, and their children. Without them many of the events would not have been experienced and the story would not have been written.

Most of all, I express my sincere appreciation and my boundless admiration to Mike Johnson. He has added immeasurably to my life.

PROLOGUE

It was the night patrol coming in off duty that woke him up. The caustic ribbing in half-whispers, heavy boots on the plank floor, and the dull thumps of gear and flak jackets. He heard them foggily, and then more clearly.

"Hey, Fats, you thinking on getting us shot to pieces? What was that dumb trick you pulled?" It was light, so no one must have gotten seriously hit this time. He rolled over.

Sleep was precious in Vietnam. You hardly ever got more than four or five straight hours. You hoarded it up in seconds and minutes, snatched between night ambush and day patrol, between hole watch and guard duty, between search-and-destroy missions and more night ambush. You were perpetually tired, a kind of bone-deep weariness that settled in rapidly when you came in green and never left until you had been off-tour for months.

Mike felt sleep skittering around the edges of his mind. When had he last not been tired, or at least felt a good kind of tired instead of this deep, haunting weariness? On R-and-R in Hawaii? When he'd had malaria? Or was it before boot camp, before this endless exhausting war with the heat, the weeds, the land, searching for an enemy that was as elusive as early morning mist? You just couldn't find them. But they could find you when they wanted you; they would find only one or two of you, then you would be one or two fewer. They would drop a grenade on you or ambush the front two guys and vanish, and you never saw them. The jungle was their weapon, even more than the grenades and the rifles. You were so tangled up in swamp, and so wet, rotting, and hot, so grimy and infected by the leaves and the grass and the mold and the bugs that you couldn't fight. It was the land that exhausted you, defeated you.

Home in West Virginia seemed far away, so far away he couldn't taste or feel it anymore. Even in his dreams it didn't come back. Home. Would he ever see it again? He turned over again. Sleep. Precious sleep.

Vietnam

1
Toward a Different Education

Mike sat, back jammed up against the rock, long legs bent loosely at the knees, propping his forearms so his large, bony hands dangled. One held the paperback. It was November 1965, and even though the rock was warm behind him and the Utah sun felt hot in his hair, the wind had a cold bite.

A hawk came circling up the canyon below him, riding the endless winds. Beyond the mouth of the canyon Mike could see part of the university he attended. Attended—that was a joke. This was his second year and he'd come back to night school at Provo's Brigham Young University to improve his grades so he could be accepted again as a daytime student. Too much time hiking, hunting, running off with whomever—but mostly himself—to climb the mountains or to play baseball. He sent home to West Virginia more photographs of Rock Canyon and baseball games and cloud lines on the mountains than he did reports on school. His dad had known! That night as Mike and Mom had sat at the kitchen table working out a schedule to juggle Chemistry 105, English, religion, basketball, and a dance class if he could get it, his dad had stood back shaking his head. And after a year of turning surgical tubing into fire hoses to shoot into the open windows of the next dorm and throwing snowballs down on passers-by and borrowing a 1965 Buick to impress the Homecoming dates, and writing home for money and counting the days, and endless hours practicing to make the frosh baseball team—after all this he had gone home on the train to West Virginia with a dollar in his pocket, a pack on his back, and failing grades.

After a summer in the railroad yard chalking coal cars so they would get coupled to the right train, and playing hours of family ballgames, he'd come back to prove up, to be someone.

Only the first thing Mike did was to buy a beautiful 264 Winchester magnum with tuition money and head up the canyons.

The hawk was higher now. Mike tipped his head back, squinting against the sun. All the sky and all the wind and just two taut wings. Mike shifted, stretched out one leg, and opened *The Green Berets* again. He wasn't reading it so much as weighing it like a decision, hefting it to see its balance and shape, and sighting along its ideas. It spelled adventure, disciplined pride and freedom, men who were at home in the hills and trees, men who could handle themselves anywhere.

The hawk had dropped down over the opposite ridge. The Green Berets were in Vietnam helping people who couldn't help themselves. Making freedom. They were men.

Mike stood up abruptly, jamming the book into his back pocket. He didn't have to decide until he'd seen the recruiter and asked him some more questions. Meantime, there was an entire afternoon of sunlight and wind, the feel of sweat drying cold under his flannel shirt, and the stretch of long muscles against rock. It was good to be up here, alive, alone.

The recruiter's window was filled with posters of marine action. Mike read them all. "The Few, The Proud, The Marines." "The United States Marines. The United States' Best." A man with his head bent into the wind jostled him. "Victory Is Always Ours."

One of the posters curled away from the window, leaving brittle, brown tape marks. A dead fly lay on its back on the dusty ledge of the window. Mike read the posters again. Mom would be upset. She wanted him to go to school, graduate, get a good job. Dad had been a marine, a good one, but he wouldn't want Mike to join, either.

Mike waggled his jaw at his dim reflection in the window and automatically ran his fingers and thumb down his chin, double-checking for whiskers. His hair was longer than his dad liked it. Marines had really short hair. Mike rubbed his, staring into the poster of the solemn young face under a white dress hat.

Inside it was dark and smelled of floor polish. There were flags and a lot of bright pamphlets in a wooden wall stand. Two floor tiles were loose and cracked at the edges. The marine recruiting officer looked up from his desk. "Can I help you?"

"Ah—yes sir. I'm Mike Johnson. I called yesterday and um . . ."

"Oh, yes." The officer stood up and held out his right hand. The wrinkles at the elbows of his khaki shirt straightened out.

"Please, Mike, sit down. Now, what can I do for you?"

It took only about fifteen minutes. It would take two days to call home.

The apartment was quiet when Mike got back, the quiet of an empty place. He closed the front door with a backward kick and listened a moment. Maybe George was catching a fast nap in the bedroom if he wasn't at work or in classes.

"Hey, anybody home?"

He shrugged at the quiet and went to double-check the bedroom. He snapped on the desk lamp and a small pool of light spilled over his math books and the paper sticking out of them. They were a little dusty.

He flopped down on the bed. What would Mom and Dad say? There was the four-month deferment, so he didn't have to go in until February. He could go home, but still . . . His rifle case was in a corner, a lone, dim-shadowed thing. He could shoot pretty well. They'd been hunting often enough, he and Steve and Papa, his grandfather. Neal was still too little, but he sometimes accompanied them on fishing trips.

The quilt was too lumpy under his back. It was too quiet. He swung his legs over the edge and got up. What class did George have today—biology, English? Or was he at work? He should be home by now.

Mike wandered out to the living room. He'd shot a deer a year ago. They'd hiked furiously up to where it had fallen after he'd fired. The hole in its solid brown hide was neat and round with only a little blood. Its eyes were open, glazed, dead, and its lower lip dragged on the ground so that the bottom teeth showed the gray edge of the tongue. There was still a little wisp of green caught in its teeth.

"Hey, man, what's happening?" George shimmied his backpack of books down off his shoulders, then wiggled out of his coat before he sat down and propped his feet up on the coffee table by Mike's.

Mike grinned and folded the magazine up in one hand. "Guess what—just guess what I did today."

"Oh, man. I come home from beating my brains out and Johnson wants to play guessing games." George slapped his forehead and slumped down, closing his eyes in mock despair. "Never fear. I need very little brain to know what you did." He squinted over at Mike. "You called Miss Universe for a date and the stupid chick accepted."

The *Outdoor Life* flapped George in the chest as Mike lunged off the couch and across the table to grab at him before he could get out of the chair. They scuffled furiously for a few minutes, madly wrestling each other. The chair tipped over. George gave a playful gasp and squawk and another couple of futile heaves.

"Okay, okay." George eased back, looking up at him smiling. "Miss Universe accepted because she knew what a dude you are—" Mike sat up, freeing George.

"And because she knew I had too much homework!" Mike grinned.

"Johnson, nothing you do surprises me. Before you grin your monkey face off, lay it on me."

Mike grinned again. "I joined the marines."

George propped up on his elbows and stared. "You're kidding."

"Nope. Signed, sealed, and delivered." Mike raised his arms up and pillowed them snugly behind his head.

"Mike, you really serious, man?"

"Yeah, I went down today and joined. I got a four-month deferment so I go in in February—boot camp, and then the real stuff."

George lay down again. "Well, how do you like that?" with soft amazement and then again, slower, "Well, how do you like that?"

And after a minute, "What did your parents say?"

Mike frowned. "Didn't tell them yet. I gotta figure out what to say. George—" He came up to his feet in a crouch. "Let's walk down to the park. I want to talk about—oh, you know, stuff like going there and what I should tell Mom and Dad."

Toward a Different Education

Harry and Marian Johnson with their family, 1967 —
Michael (top left), Stephen, Neal, Lynn

George got up and reached for his coat. "Sure, okay, sure." He grinned faintly. "I mean the only other thing I have to do is about thirty-eight hours of homework."

Mike slapped him on the shoulder and went to get his own coat.

They'd gone walking, talking until dark. They'd stopped at a Hi-Spot for a hamburger and chocolate shake and talked about shooting at a man; and then they walked, talked about whether war was evil, about boot camp, about the four-month student deferment. Then they sat on the edge of a park bench with their legs stuck out in front, shoulders shoved up against the back of the bench, hands in their pockets, and talked about Mike's dad and how he hardly ever said anything about the war. Sometimes they looked at each other, but mostly they walked or sat and looked straight ahead while they talked.

Back in the apartment, George had one last question: "Mike, what if you get shot? I mean—" George hesitated. "What if you get killed?"

The four months at home slipped into each other rapidly, blurring their brightness together like the edges of water colors. The single moments were the clearest. Mom in a pool of sunlight, turning hot loaves out on the table, laughing when Mike tore off a hunk, gulping it down, so steamy sweet it didn't need butter or honey. Sleepy three-year-old Lynn curling her arm around his neck and snuggling her curly head into his shoulder. He'd meant to tickle her. Instead he stood very still, cradling her, swallowing.

He played football in the late afternoon with cousin David, fourteen, and Neal and Steve, ages six and twelve, sweating and laughing, their breaths frosty puffs. Mike picked up Neal on his shoulder with a block that sent his brother slamming back to the ground and knocked the ball out of his arms. He bent over and scooped up the football with one hand. Neal came bouncing up and rammed Mike, choking mad that he'd lost the ball and that he was so little that Mike could put him down with ease.

Steve ran all the way down the lot with David after him into the edge of the twilight. Mike ripped off one glove and shoved it in his pocket. He could feel the leather, rough and curved snugly in his palm. He sidestepped, picking up momentum as he turned, bringing the ball up over his shoulder and back. His arm flung forward and the ball snapped away from his hand in a long, clean arch.

Mike stood and watched it rise, whirling swiftly up and then in a long reaching arch down. He could barely see David and Steve in the shadows, their shouts a little muffled.

There was a whoop from downfield and the thump of David cutting into Steve, then the hard boot of a football being kicked, and he came alert, looking above the dark treeline. The ball spiraled down from the navy sky. His arms and body reached and then followed the ball into his midsection, welcoming it and pulling it in.

He was running; Steve and David came racing for him, but he twisted around and by them, glorying in the speed, the unstoppability, the power. With each step every muscle from his hip and thigh and calf reached out for the other end of the field. There was a star just above the dark treeline and under the low cloud level, and he fixed his eyes on it and ran for it.

They swaggered home, Mike in the middle with an elbow bent around each boy's neck and the football tucked on Steve's hip.

Cathy was a cute girl—not pretty, but pert and cute. Mike had dated her quite a bit when he first got home because almost everyone else was still away at school. Christmas break had turned into one party after another, the girls admiring, awed, flatteringly anxious about the danger. Mike talked about the Green Berets and fighting for freedom and liberating people from communism. He felt heroic. The girls fell in love quickly, but then Christmas vacation was over and they went back to school and he saw Cathy more often.

It was snowing and they went for a walk after bowling. Cathy stuck her tongue out, trying to catch one of the heavy snow flakes. "Watch the snow—a lot of calories in those flakes."

She grinned impishly at him. "You should try to enjoy the snow while you've got it. I mean, it doesn't snow where you're going. Does it?"

He shrugged. "I don't know. I guess not."

She took his hand and tugged him out from under a tree. "Well then, stand here and catch some snow."

Mike looked up at the snow feathering out of the dark sky. Suddenly he felt a thousand miles away. The trees were harsh black lines muffled under the snow, which turned silver in the street lights and gold under the porch lights. The flakes melted on his face. He felt the wetness as though it were someone else's skin. Cathy stood beside him, her face turned up, snowflakes piling on her eyelashes and short dark hair. Vietnam. What would it be? He'd been waiting for it but not thinking about it. Now it was here, cutting him off from his own skin, separating him from Cathy.

He saw his hand go out and touch her. She turned willingly into his arms and he kissed her, tasting the warmth of her mouth and the cold of the snow, and feeling himself dark and apart inside.

2

"The Few, the Proud..."

February 1966. Outside the marine recruiter's office one boy's parents stood on the sidewalk by their blue station wagon. The mother had gray hair squashed up under a fuzzy hat. She was clutching the inside of her boy's sleeve with one hand and pressing a crumpled lace-edged handkerchief across her mouth and nose. His father, a slight man, was hunched into his coat looking abandoned and dazed.

Inside, Mike watched a skinny boy whose knees hardly rippled the front of his pants. The pale lashes of his red-rimmed eyes disappeared when he turned his head into the light. Had he been crying? Probably not, Mike decided.

The room was full of silent faces. They shifted every time the door opened to let in the cold and another recruit, measuring the new one against themselves, against the marines, absorbing him into the group. Then they turned back to the door.

Finally, the boy outside slipped his mother into the car, flicked a nervous good-bye, and straightened toward the building. All eyes followed him through the door. He flushed and tossed a mock salute.

Outside, three gray station wagons pulled up to the curb. The marine officer took his clipboard to the door.

"Anderson, Richard L."
"Cardow, Evan Carl."
"Carlisle, Tom."

The recruits filed by holding their bags.

"Duffey, Patrick."

"Move it. Move it." The marine officer called one name twice, then muttered something to the man next to him.

"Johnson, Michael."

This was it.

The red brick buildings of Fort Douglas had commanded the hillside above the University of Utah for a hundred years. The station wagons waited only until the recruits jumped onto the slush and gravel, then gunned out. The officers, no less impatient, hustled the recruits up the stairs, snapping at one who paused to look at the building.

Inside, the officers checked the bags, cut the recruits into four alphabetical groups, and ran them past four secretaries who never looked up as they typed the new files. Then the boys were whisked through a relay of physicians who tapped and prodded, who shone lights into throats, eyes, ears, noses, and who stripped them to the skin. "Move, move, move." "You there. In line. Don't let me see you out again." "You! You've got nothing to talk about." Some marine personnel yelled, some bellowed, some snapped.

After a day in line, the recruits marched to the barracks. The sergeant, never looking up from his clipboard, stepped an exact pace from one bunk to the next.

"Anderson, top; Barkley, bottom. Johnson, top; Lukow, bottom." Down the line. Each recruit moved to his bunk and stood silently. The missing recruit was still on the list.

"You have fifteen minutes to get into your bunks before the lights go out. We'll wake you up early." The sergeant stiffly marched the length of the barracks.

"Any questions?"

No one spoke.

"Good. Hit the sack." He turned, pulled at the door, and left.

At first no one moved. Then here and there tentative conversations sprang up.

"Man, am I tired." The boy next to Mike shook his head, unbuckling his belt.

"It's all that listening. I never listened so hard in my life."

"Yeah, I know." Mike slipped off his shoes and unzipped his case.

"My mom would be proud. I never listened like this before."

Mike smiled. "Yeah."

Mike climbed under his scratchy, damp blanket, but the sheets quickly warmed around him. Mom would have made him brush his teeth. She always made sure of such things, getting up to fix breakfast before Dad left for work at five and then again with Mike just after six so he could eat before his early morning seminary class; making dentist appointments; packing food, clean shirts, and three pairs of warm socks when they went hunting.

The light went out.

"Hey! I wasn't ready." Then there was silence.

"I should say my prayers," Mike thought to himself. His feet were finally warm again. But he slipped to his knees and tried to wrap the blanket around his front.

The next day the green recruits flew out of Salt Lake City, heading for the Marine Corps Recruit Depot in San Diego.

It was evening when the plane taxied into the airport. One of the recruits suddenly leaned forward and looked out of the window.

"Man, oh man! Look what's coming."

Several canvas-covered trucks were pulling onto the runway. NCOs climbed out of the cab and the back of each truck. They stood there waiting. The plane had scarcely stopped when the door opened and a second lieutenant stood in the aisle.

"All right, scumheads. You think you want to be marines? Then move like one."

The recruits scrambled for their flight bags. A skinny blond kid close to the front waited in his seat for the others. The NCO was on him in a second.

"You deaf? I said, 'Move it!' "

The kid shrugged and started to stand. The officer grabbed him by the front of the shirt.

"All right, fleabrain, you stand. You stand here and don't move until I say. And when I say 'move'—you'd better fly."

He snapped back to the group who had frozen, watching. They jostled into an untidy line. Mike could feel his muscles stiffen as they climbed down the stairs into the verbal volley.

"Tough guys? When I'm done with you, you'll wish you were home hanging onto Mama's apron strings."

"The Few, the Proud..."

People were watching, even some girls his own age. Mike felt sick and stupid. His fingers trembled as he climbed into one of the trucks. A black guy accidentally bumped him and muttered, "Sorry, man," his head down.

Immediately an NCO appeared. "Shut up, boy. You got nothing to say, and when you do, I'll tell you."

They sat on benches inside the trucks, looking at their feet. The black guy sat with his head down, his face stiff. Mike wanted to reach over, shake his shoulder, say something, but he didn't.

Before the trucks stopped at the Marine Corps Recruit Depot, an officer was unlatching the tailgate and screaming, "Get out. Why don't you go home and send your grandmother instead?"

Mike jumped onto asphalt painted with yellow footprints.

"Get on the yellow footprints." Mike jumped for the nearest pair. He tried to match his toe and heel to the toe and heel of the footprint, but his toe spilled over the edge.

"Don't move, don't talk, and if you have to breathe, don't let me see you do it." The marine bit the words off without moving his clenched teeth. Rolls of red skin lapped over his collar. Three sergeants circled the group, watching.

"It must be about eight or nine o'clock," Mike thought. He slowly twisted his watch toward his body and stared ahead, fixing on the windows of the building. He started to lower his eyelashes a fraction of an inch at a time.

"Maggot! Skinhead!"

Mike jumped at the rough bark but took a careful breath when he realized the sergeant was looking at someone in the last row.

"Don't you move, maggot. Don't you let me see you move. Come on, boy, do it, move." Another sergeant was baiting a boy to Mike's right. He slapped him, then circled the group, again hungry for the slightest movement. A bull sergeant stepped in front of the group.

"All right—haircuts! Start with the first one in this corner. You run through, scum, and I mean *run*!"

Three barbers stood shoe-top deep in hair, hot clippers humming. As soon as one haircut was finished, the barber swung the chair around. One recruit jumped out and another in before the chair stopped in front of the barber. A haircut took only about ten seconds.

"There you go, son." The barber whisked the recruit out of his chair. Mike climbed into the old, cracked red chair. The barber didn't even bother to tie a cloth around his neck. He simply dragged the clippers from Mike's forehead, across his head, and all the way down his neck.

Tears welled up in Mike's eyes. The buzz vibrated in his ears, and the clippers seemed to tear instead of cut. The barber smelled of cigar smoke and sweet soap, and he was humming inside his throat.

The clipper buzzed two or three times around each ear and up the back of his neck, and then the barber bumped Mike out of the chair. Mike stumbled over a cord and headed toward the door gingerly, exploring a nick on his neck. A sergeant grabbed him by the arm and shook him towards the door. "Get in there and change your clothes, scum. Now!"

The big room was a confusion of benches, boxes, un-gummed labels, clothes. Someone called, "Johnson, Michael," and shoved a tight bundle of green into his hands. Mike started to set the bundle down on the bench, then realized everyone was frantically stripping, dropping into boxes the things they were wearing and hurrying for the showers.

Mike began ripping off his shirt. The bark of the sergeants never stopped. He threw his clothes, wallet, and watch into a box and looked for a towel, poking hopefully at the green fatigues.

"Move it, move it!"

The showers were blasting the new white-tiled walls. Mike pushed into the crowd and the icy, driving water almost knocked him over. A sliver of hard soap drifted over the cement floor by the drain, and he bent to pick it up, bumping someone else in the shower behind him.

A sergeant was yelling, "Get out, get out. Think you got all day?" Hurriedly, Mike ran the soap over his head and chest, skimming down each leg. He stood well away from the pounding ice water, only ducking under to rinse off. His feet were cold on the cement, but the water felt good on his stinging head.

Mike stepped out, spotting a pile of towels and grabbing one as he headed back to his clothes. A sudden unreasoning panic seized him. The marines would march him out of the room whether he was dressed or not, and he wouldn't have any boots or pants on.

"Dry off!"

"Get back in there and shower, and I mean you soap until I see the lather in your ears."

Mike ducked his head lower, drying furiously, and grabbed for his green pile. He wasn't even sure this was his bundle, but it didn't seem to matter. He yanked on socks and underwear and pulled on his pants, hopping a few times on his left foot while his right foot fumbled through the pant leg. He didn't zip the zipper but looked frantically for a pair of boots. The boots were too big and so were the pants and shirts. He looked around. Everybody's shirts and pants seemed to be too big.

Mike wondered if he could walk in his boots without stumbling. A wrinkle in one sock was hurting his heel, but he was afraid he'd be caught with one boot off, so he did nothing about it.

He hastily scrambled through his box to make sure everything was there. Then he folded down the top flaps, stuck the label with his home address on the lid, and hurried to join his group in front of the shower building.

NCOs pushed the new recruits at a dead run toward the Quonset barracks about eight blocks away. In front of one of the steel mushrooms, the officers yelled, "Halt!"

One sergeant, a big man with turkey jowls under his chin, moved down the line counting off recruits for each Quonset hut. In front of Mike, he stopped.

"What's your name?"

Mike swallowed and let his eyes drift to the sergeant's.

"Mike Johnson."

The sergeant flared back and jabbed at Mike with his finger. "You're not Mike Johnson. There is no such person! You are Private Johnson." The fingers poked his nose. "Do you understand, Private Johnson?"

"Yes, sir!"

"Now, who are you?"

"I'm Private Johnson." Mike's voice was higher than usual.

The sergeant narrowed his eyes.

"What did you say?"

Mike's stomach jumped. "I just told you. I'm Private Johnson."

The sergeant moved closer to Mike with each word, his jaw jutting.

"Listen very carefully, stupid. I am not 'you.' I am 'sir.' You say 'sir' before you talk to me and 'sir' after you talk to me. Never say 'you,' because that's a female sheep."

Mike could see the sergeant's lips tightening and loosening over his clenched teeth as he spoke.

"You never say 'I want to talk to you.' You say 'Sir, the private requests permission to speak to the drill instructor, sir!'"

Mike gulped. Dad had taught him to say "yes, sir" at home. "Sir, yes, sir, I understand, sir." It was quick and firm.

"Good." The sergeant eased back.

"You think you can handle these barracks?"

"Sir, yes, sir."

"Okay, private. You're in charge. If anything happens, it's your neck. You keep your nose clean and you keep their noses clean, too."

"Sir, yes, sir!" Mike could almost hear George's voice, faintly mocking.

The sergeant yelled the group in through the doors. Bunks lined the bare walls, two bulbs glaring down on the splintered wood floors.

"You have twenty seconds to make your bunks so tight I can bounce a quarter off them. Now!"

Finally, it was quiet and dark. Mike wondered if anyone else was feeling the same dazed ache. He kept remembering the box with clothes that fit, his driver's license, the pictures of Cathy and his family. The last of his mother's chocolate-chip cookies had been tossed in the trash. *They've got me completely.*

"Hey, Johnson?" The whisper came from the next top bunk.

"Yeah?"

"What do you think? I mean, did you expect this?"

"Sort of. My dad was a marine."

"Man, I didn't know."

The kid in the bunk below now joined in.

"Man, I don't know, I mean I just don't know."

Mike shifted, leaned down on the edge, and whispered, "Hi. Who are you?"

"I'm not real sure any more. Seems like I've just disappeared, like that staff sergeant said."

"Yeah," Mike yawned, "I guess."

Soon other names were swapped and feelings about the day turned over, compared, first in whispers, then more normal talking, an occasional muffled laugh.

Suddenly, the door crashed open, swinging violently on its hinges, and the bright, naked bulbs flared on.

"Out of the rack! Get out!" The whole room was furiously shaping into two rows of white boxer shorts. The sergeant kicked the more casual recruits, shrieking, "Out! Out!"

"What do you think you're doing? When I said sleep, I meant sleep." He raged up and down the aisle.

"You think you're tough? You want to be marines?" He stuck his jaw into one face after another, yelling, daring them to blink or talk back, slapping a couple. It lasted ten minutes. Mike did not join in the few whispered conversations afterward. Through the confusion and turmoil, his exhausted body won sleep immediately.

"It's five o'clock. Out of the sack, out, out! You've got two minutes to get those bunks made tight and you dressed for breakfast."

Mike grabbed for his boots, hopping into his pants while he pulled at the covers.

"Put on those uniforms like men, or go home to Mother where she can dress you."

On the sidewalk they did push-ups—thirty-five straight with the sergeant counting and yelling at anyone who hesitated. It was still dark. Mike's arms trembled. He moved his hands out a little further so he could keep going and concentrated on keeping his nose off the sidewalk.

Then they were up, running in place. "Get those knees up, get those knees up." A fat kid next to Mike doubled over, groaning and grasping his side. Mike ran hard, keeping his elbows in close to his sides and his hands in easy fists. He thought about running with a football, like at home.

The sergeant screamed again, and they took off, blindly following him. Mike opened up his stride. But his boots were only partly laced; they were heavy and chafed at his ankles. People were falling out, hunched forward, holding their stomachs, curled into balls. One recruit was throwing up in great heaves as he ran. Mike's lungs hurt. He could feel his right sock disappearing into his boot, felt the raw flesh. The sergeant gave only one rest while a recruit who had passed out came around, one cheek smudged from the dirt where he fell. Then it was more push-ups until the sergeant gathered in the stragglers.

Finally the sergeant shaped them into lines to march to chow. Mike tucked in his shirt again, pulled his belt tight, and pulled his right boot off to straighten the sock. He laced the boot tight this time. He felt much more comfortable as they ran the whole way.

A neat sign stood at the entrance: Take All You Want, But Eat All You Take. Mike picked up a wet, hot tray. Most of the recruits were loading up half a dozen pancakes, drenched in syrup, four eggs, two cartons of milk, a box or two of cold cereal. The cook slopped creamed eggs over Mike's hand as he came through the line. Mike glared but bit his tongue and reached for two pieces of dry toast. He sat down with a knot of men he recognized and picked up his fork.

"Sit at attention." They all dropped their forks. "You'll stay that way until I give you an order." The NCO waited, glaring around at them. "Ready, eat, and I don't mean eat until you're comfortable. You will eat everything you've taken and eat it fast. Don't talk. This is the marines, not a ladies Sunday brunch."

They shoved, cramming the food in, swallowing it half-chewed, trying to clear their plates before the sergeant came back. He was running squads out of the Quonset hut. Mike finished before Sergeant Hubbard came back. As he stood with his tray, he noticed a fat recruit staring at his eggs, lips already puffed and bloated. Mike followed a marine with bloused pants through the dishwashing line, dumping paper garbage and dipping his tray and dishes into garbage cans full of hot water with soap, hot water with disinfectant, rinse water.

Outside the group milled on the road. Soon the fat kid came swaying out of the hall. He washed his tray and jabbed it in the disinfectant, then turned and ran behind the nearest hut.

They worked some more in the afternoon but finally took a break. Mike wrote home about the flight out, the time they went to bed and got up. But he couldn't think of anything else he wanted Mom and Dad to know.

The recruits received their rifles, M-14s, that evening. They spent an hour and a half breaking down the rifle, learning how to carry, clean, and take care of it. A dirty rifle in Vietnam could mean your life. Here it would mean the guardhouse. The instructors also outlined the schedule for the next few weeks. No one just leaves the marines, they explained. "We run you through basic again and again until you pass, are given an undesirable discharge, or go crazy repeating the same thing over and over again. You can be in basic six months, or a year. So shut up, and don't screw up!"

Three weeks after they'd come in green, Sergeant Sands and Platoon Commander Hubbard took them out to run laps around the half-mile track. As he ran, Mike could feel the sweat seeping out of his temples and his shoulder blades. After three laps, the guide, who was the honor man of the platoon, began to falter. He was shaking and white-knuckled. Mike, running next to him, scooped up the heavy flag before it could touch the ground and sprinted to the head of the formation. He felt suddenly, crazily happy, and he carried it as long as he could before passing it on.

They finished the laps and came off to the side of the track, gasping. Heavy, irregular sweat patches blotted most of their backs and under their arms. Mike wiped his face, wondering how hot it would be in Vietnam.

"Get to the ropes!"

Mike dug his feet into the sand next to the thirty-foot rope. He crouched, tensing up for the spring, wiping his palms on the seat of his trousers. He wanted to win this one, but he remembered the pull of muscle and tendon in the forearms of one of the squad leaders who had handwrestled down each man in his squad.

"Go."

Mike flung at the rope, clawed, caught, and then pushed into smooth action so that the rope wouldn't swing wildly. The rope was prickly, stiff in his palms, scraping at his hands. His breath pounded harsh in his throat and sweat stung his eyes. His upper palm smacked the wood.

"Johnson first, Andrews second, Thomas . . ."

Mike stared, then laughed, still panting, swinging back and forth a little on the rope. The rope burned through his hands as he slid down. About half way he let his feet drop away from the rope, hung there. The sand cushioned him as he fell, staggered, but caught his balance. The next squad members were already lined up at the ropes. He went over to the side and whistled and yelled for his squad. They lost, but he had won.

"Private Johnson."

Mike jumped up. Sergeant Hubbard motioned with a jerk of his head. Mike walked over.

"Yes, sir."

Sergeant Hubbard held out the guide's armband. "Take this and go get in front of the platoon."

"Sir?"

"I believe you heard me."

"Yes, sir!" Mike took the armband, stretching it up over his sleeve.

The sergeant hunched his shoulder, looked past him.

"On your feet, everyone, move it. We're not on a vacation."

Sergeant Sands came by Mike's post. They chatted briefly about what the squad was to do the next day. Then Sergeant Sands shifted and looked squarely at Mike.

"You know, private, you're never last in anything." He tapped Mike's armband. "Now you've got it. You'd better keep it."

The next week they went to Camp Pendleton, where they spent the first week at mess duty. The sergeants yelled them out of bed at two o'clock in the morning so they could stare sleepy-eyed at the stark aluminum kitchen and stir up batches of pancakes, peel potatoes, and mix cans of powdered eggs with milk. They kept up with the line of hungry men in green, but just barely. Then they'd scrape down the grills, wash everything, empty the garbage, clean up the mess, and start over on lunch. But Mike finally got enough to eat and usually got to supervise rather than scrub or stir.

Mike received letters from Neal (painstakingly copied over) and from Barbara at BYU. He poured over the delicate paper, ruffling its crispness in his fingers. It was six pages long, both sides covered with curving sloped lines. He had to be in bed by nine o'clock, but his bunk was right next to the door; so he stayed up a few nights, lying on his stomach, propping his elbows under the wool blanket, writing by the green light of the exit sign. He printed letters to the kids at home, wrote Barbara, and doodled a birthday card for his mom. Some of the guys had no families. Mike wondered how they could get through with no one to write to. No one to get mail from.

The next Sunday he went to church, sat with a dozen men, and felt awkward, irreverent to be there in combat boots. The chaplain asked him to pass the sacrament. The curved metal handle of the bread tray was cool and silk smooth in his fingers. Being in church made him feel closer to the countless shadowy Sundays spent sitting with his family on wooden church benches. Even when he felt bored and put his head on the bench so he could sleep, the solid sense of family had been around him.

He passed the broken bread to each marine, listened to the prayer, then offered them the tray of tiny water cups. He took his own slowly. The chapel seemed so quiet. Yesterday the rifle instructor had picked him out of the ranks to demonstrate "snapping in," how to get your arm wrapped and locked through the rifle strap and the rifle into your shoulder so you could shoot dead at five hundred yards. Locked into that position you were rock steady.

He shifted on the chair, laced his fingers, and rested them below his belt. The chaplain was talking about growing beyond the hard things, taking the dirt and coarseness and building on top of it. He talked about how to be strong without being a bully, and how to be a leader of men who had values different from your own.

Mike's mind drifted just a little. He remembered the little talk—no, the little speech—his bishop had given him just before he left West Virginia for boot camp.

"Mike, you're going to be rubbing shoulders with men whose background and training are very different from your own. Many will use coarse language, alcohol, and drugs, and may have loose morals. Keep praying and remember who you are, son, and you'll be fine."

It was a funny thing about boot camp! Mike could tell the bishop had never been to one. No one used drugs, and smoking wasn't allowed; some drank beer, but only as a thirst-quencher. There were no beer parties in boot camp. Mike's desire to use booze or tobacco was no greater here than at home, and it had been no problem at home. He had found himself cussing some, however, and he decided he needed to work on that one. The bishop had been right in one area, however; prayer had been a help, a great help. Mike was grateful he knew how to pray and to whom.

After the meeting, Mike loitered. He didn't know these men but they shared something. They wanted to talk to each other, and lingered awkwardly about their chairs. In the squad Mike worked with other guys, grumbled with them, ran in fierce competition with them, ate and slept and showered with them, made a platoon with them. But the platoon men would never be in the sinew and bone of his life.

On the first day on the rifle range Sergeant Hubbard let them blouse their trousers. He showed them how to catch the pant leg in the black cloth elastic band so there was an even blouse around the boot and so the pant leg was held securely around the leg at the top of the boot. Now mosquitoes and dirt couldn't work down into the boot or the leg. They looked more like marines without their pants flapping down over their boots. Mike was starting to feel like one, too.

They watched the marksmanship instructor snap to position, winding his arm through the gun sling and forcing the gun flat onto his shoulder so that his arm was rock steady. Mike lay in the hot dust with his rifle and felt as if the ball and socket of his shoulder were tearing loose. He remembered playing baseball with his dad; even with his hand sweaty and raw inside the mitt, Mike had begged him to keep throwing. Mike had pounded a basketball until he could switch hands without letting the ball bobble and glance off into the corner. Snapping the rifle must be the same—practice until the movement is unconscious in your muscles and nerves.

Mike coughed, wanted water, coughed again. His forearm was limp, rubbery, and shaking when he released the rifle from firing position. But as soon as he snapped it in, the arm was rock hard again. Fascinated, he snapped in again. His arm was not part of him but was guided and controlled by the rifle. He sat up, propped his rifle across his legs, and slapped his fingers across his thigh. The tingling, limp sensation went away. He wondered when they would use real ammunition and real targets.

For a week they shot empty. The marksmanship instructor would position them around a huge white cylinder with black dots scattered up and down its smooth sides. The squads would snap in, sight the black, and shoot, the firing pins falling with empty clicks on the chambers. Sometimes they shot for two straight hours, over and over, sighting up, down, and straight on. When an arm went to sleep, the recruit unwrapped it, pinched and shook it to get the blood and nerves moving again, and then wrapped up in his rifle and shot again, measuring the sun in the empty clicks of the M-14. They ran laps and shot again. They went dirty and tired to the mess hall, ran more laps, and cleaned each weapon carefully before they drew sleep around their exhaustion. Then morning came and they were shooting again.

The new marines soon got their Phase II training clothing—dress greens and khaki. Even though the lines moved fairly rapidly, it took all day. The uniforms were new, pressed, crisp, and they fit. Mike looked in the mirror. The newness was stiff across his chest and neck. He cocked the black rim of his hat. This was the first time he'd worn a tie since before boot camp, and the snug collar felt strange around his neck. He threw his heels together, so the crease ran straight down his legs, and held a salute, shoulders back, chest out—like a marine, he thought. Mike made sure his uniform hung in his locker so it wouldn't wrinkle or crease.

One afternoon, Sergeant Hubbard called them off the rifle range to run relays to pick out the fastest squad in the platoon. They sprinted up and down the sandy areas, through net obstacles and tires. The squads were faster, smoother, tighter than they had ever been, and the competition was bitter.

Mike ran hard each time, lifting his knees cleanly over each obstacle. He kept his mouth loose and tried to breathe evenly, concentrating on the contest and speed, so many running steps to each breath in and each breath out. He won and won again, springing from his crouched position at the starting gun, until only he and a black kid from another squad were left. The two of them lined up, toed off, ready to go.

"C'mon, Johnson."

"Take him, man, do it!"

The squad was shouting feverishly. Mike tensed as the sergeant raised the gun, tightening his finger on the trigger. A wild thought flashed across Mike's mind, and as the gun cracked, he crashed like a defensive end into the black kid. Mike landed easily, but the black kid rolled on one shoulder, the jolt jarring his shoulder, head, back, and legs against the ground. Mike was up and running for the finish line like a football player on a clear field. Grit from the fall worked around Mike's teeth, but he waited to spit until he had crossed the finish line, yards ahead of the other man. He stopped, running his tongue over his teeth and working up saliva from the back of his mouth. He spat, then grinned. His squad was uncontested; they were in the marines.

Mike jogged by the black kid and laughed. "Hey, you okay, guy?"

The kid was rubbing his shoulder. "What's wrong with you, Johnson? Can't you race clean?"

Mike shrugged. "All in good fun."

The squads fell out for mess hall. A couple of men slapped Mike lightly and mumbled, "Good race." Most were quiet, jogging or walking through the dirt and the thin afternoon shadows.

Later, Mike was called to the duty hut. The others pretended not to notice as he got up, smoothed his pants down, and left the room. He knocked on the duty-hut door.

"Sir, Private Johnson requests permission to speak to the drill instructor, sir."

"Enter."

He stepped up into the hall, shut the door, and snapped to attention.

"Sir, Private Johnson reporting as ordered, sir."

Sergeant Hubbard sat at a desk facing the door. Mike looked at the gray cinderblock wall behind the sergeant's head.

"At ease."

Mike moved one leg into a stiff spread position and crossed his hands behind his back. He clenched his right fist, waiting.

The sergeant sat back in his chair.

"So, you play the hero, win the big race, and you're a big man with the platoon now. Big man." He got up and leaned over the desk.

Mike's lips were stiff.

"Are you listening to me?"

"Sir. Yes, sir."

"You had better be."

The sergeant's voice dripped ice water.

"That stupid move of yours hurt Private Jackson's shoulder. Now he won't shoot well on the rifle range. That will pull down the whole platoon. That kid will have that mark the rest of his stay in the Marine Corps."

"Sir, I didn't mean—"

"Shut up."

Sergeant Hubbard came around the desk and circled Mike. "Johnson, you're nothing but garbage in this squad. You get to the tail end, Charlie. You bring up the rear. Someone else will be platoon guide."

The sergeant held out one red hand and snapped the fingers under Mike's nose, as if he were calling his dog. Mike worked the guide armband down off his left arm and held it out. The sergeant tossed it on the desk contemptuously.

"Now you get out of here. Dismissed."

Mike turned, fumbling at the doorknob. He swung it shut behind him, shaking now, but he marched with his heels hitting the ground crisply. He'd blown it. He'd blown it. Stupid! Stupid! The sergeant had called him "Charlie," a name for Viet Cong. What could he write to Mom and Dad now? But then he wished that they were here or that he was there in the kitchen with the smell of roast cooking and the muddy slush dripping off his dad's boots in the corner.

The barracks quieted when he came in. He opened his locker, sifted out pen and paper, and sat down on his bed, pretending to write a letter. Gradually the voices around him picked up.

Later that night he went out looking for the black kid. The guy wasn't in his bunk. Mike wandered around the hospital unit and the mess hall. Then he rounded the corner between two Quonset huts and met him.

The marine started to step past him but stopped as Mike reached swiftly up, not touching him but half-barring the way.

"Hey," Mike asked, "is your arm going to be okay?"

"Yeah."

They stood silently. Mike let his arm drop flat against his side.

"I'm sorry. I mean, man, I didn't think it would hurt."

"Yeah, well."

The black man stood waiting, not meeting his eyes. Mike shrugged.

"Sorry." He stood and watched the marine pass him. Then he went back to his own barracks.

The entire squad was tense the rest of the week. Sergeant Hubbard ran them harder, yelled more often, cut them closer. Mike tried to ignore the animosity around him and concentrated on shooting, wanting to erase the black mark on his record and to win the marksmanship award.

He lay in the dirt for hours at a time, sighting, shooting, sighting again—hitting the black center five hundred yards away nearly every time. The gun pounded into his shoulder, the metal became hot under his hands, and his trigger finger ached. After one long session at the range, Mike relaxed, eased off, and unwrapped his left arm from the gun strap. It was numb.

The next morning his arm was still numb but he went to the rifle range and shot. The numbness didn't affect his arm. It just felt odd and unattached. Finally, he stopped the range instructor.

"Sir."

"Yes, private."

Mike hesitated. "Sir, my arm has been numb since yesterday, sir." The instructor squinted at him.

"Affect your aim?"

"No, sir."

"How many hours did you spend shooting yesterday?"

"Probably four in the afternoon straight."

The instructor grunted. "You've got sling palsy from the pressure of the strap and the gun position. It'll go away eventually. In the meantime, take a few more breaks on target practice."

"Thank you, sir." Mike hesitated. The instructor turned back to his clipboard.

"Sir."

The instructor glanced up again.

"Sir, in my shooting tomorrow, will my shooting be, well, off?"

The instructor shook his head.

They would be shooting for marksmanship standings to take into the marines. A counter would stand behind each shoulder and count five points for the black center, four points for the first white outside the black center. A recruit could be ranked expert, marksman, or rifleman. Usually only one or two in a platoon made expert.

Mike began the morning well, racking up five points on nearly every shot. His arm and hand were still numb but he was hitting accurately, the bullets wanging dead center of the target.

"Good shot, good shot," echoed behind him.

"Hey, private, you got it. Expert rating. That's it."

Mike laughed and stretched his right arm. "You sure?"

"Yeah. Yeah. You got it."

Mike rolled up and snapped off his last shot, then shimmied the rifle off his arm and laid it down across one knee. Four points. The shot had barely nicked the black center

"The Few, the Proud..."

because he'd taken such an easy fast shot. But Mike didn't really care. Expert would look fine on his record.

He came up one point short. Mike stared at the rating. One point. He could have shot dead center if he had taken his time. He felt robbed. But where could the smoldering anger go?

When they returned from Camp Pendleton to the Marine Corps Depot, they were marines, with bloused trousers and starched creases in their sleeves and pant legs. Their heels hit the ground with the sharp, unified sound of a marine squad marching. They smiled at the loose trousers, half-laced boots, and almost bloody heads of the arriving platoons. Mike was quietly put back in as squad leader.

Sergeant Hubbard started showing them slides and movies of Vietnam, men crouching in holes, behind barbed wire, jumping out of helicopters, wading knee-deep in muddy water. Mike couldn't shake the slide of Huey, the giant magnesium helicopter exploding into a ball of searing flame and smoke. Sergeant Hubbard told them that the life expectancy of helicopter men in the air in Vietnam was very short, measured in days.

There were pictures of Viet Cong attacking base. Sergeants Sand and Hubbard talked and drew chalkboard diagrams and tried to explain Vietnam to privates who had never seen steamy jungles and had never shot at anything besides targets that flipped up out of the bushes. The sergeants had been there.

They drilled the platoon endlessly in formation. Mike thought more and more about graduation, because his mom and dad would be coming. He could show them around camp and tell them about missing expert and give them hugs for everybody back home. He wanted them to see him as a marine.

Nearly everyone was up early that May-morning graduation day; young men in undershirts and shorts wiping down lockers, polishing shoes until soft, curved reflections appeared. One boy returned from the showers, flipping his towel at the aisle of busy recruits. Mike had told one or two of them that his mom and dad were flying out from West Virginia, and the word had spread around the barracks. Some were amazed that they would spend the money to come so far for just part of a day, and some had whistled and teased Mike about needing his mother. Mike promised them all a taste of the best chocolate-chip cookies ever. Mom would have her hair styled stiff around her face and wear her best polyester suit. Dad's suit would smell faintly of dry cleaning. They would be proud and quiet.

Mike gave another hard swipe at his shoe and held it up to inspect the shine. He had alternated thin layers of paste and water, the water beading up on his shoes like rain on the newly waxed hood of a car. The guy on the next bunk was tucking his blanket in hard and smooth, his dog tags swinging as he bent over. He looked up, caught Mike's eye, and they both started laughing.

They shed their combat fatigues and took the crisp, starched uniforms with their hard-pressed creases out of the lockers. The paper covering the hangers crackled as they shook the uniforms off the hangers and laid them carefully on the bed. Everyone was quiet now, absorbed in buttoning their uniforms, polishing off the hat brims with the cuff of one sleeve.

Mike straightened his sleeves and tucked the long shirt smoothly around his bottom before he zipped up his trousers and buckled his belt. He fingered the buttons and the embroidered patches on his sleeves. Moving down to stand by the mirror, he flipped the tan tie over his head. Not satisfied with the first attempt, he slid the knot out and kept trying until the ends were even and flat and the knot a tight, solid weight below his Adam's apple.

Mike wondered where his parents were now. Mom had written that they intended to stay with Aunt Emma the first night and go to Disneyland to buy Mickey Mouse hats and postcards for the kids at home.

Finally, Mike lined up his squad with the rest of the platoon outside the barracks and looked them over. From the back they looked stamped from the same machine. Mike took his place as Sergeants Hubbard and Sand came out of their huts. Standing there in the sun, Mike felt himself dissolving like the heat waves into the squad, into the platoon, into the marines.

They marched to the waiting guests seated in folding chairs outside the theater. Mike saw his parents anxiously scanning the three-hundred men in khaki. His mom was whispering something in his dad's ear. Mike watched until a man two rows up moved and he couldn't see them any longer.

"The Few, the Proud..."

With parents at boot camp graduation,
May 1967

The program began with a clear bugle signaling the presentation of the colors. The recruits rose to salute; the audience rippled up, their hands over their hearts. The invocation was given and then the commanding officer, Major F. X. Quinn, presented the special awards to the honormen and experts. Mike could feel the heat in his face as he sat there, knowing he could have been receiving an expert award. One lousy point!

Back at his seat Mike listened, his head slightly down. All through boot camp he had waited for this day when the military would tell him he was a marine. It seemed strange to be here, sitting with the starch going limp between his shoulder blades.

"I assure you that these men sitting here...." Mike listened to the grand words about defending freedom. He imagined shining shores guarded with a bristle of ready M-16s. The major gestured broadly toward the platoon. "These are the marines."

Everyone applauded and kept applauding. The marines stood, and sang "From the Halls of Montezuma to the Shores of Tripoli," and then Mike was standing with an arm around each parent, hugging them and pushing back on the wetness at the corners of his eyes.

They took pictures, standing on the brick steps under the red and gold banner that read: "Your Corps. Your Country. Your God. *Semper Fidelis.*" Mike's dad also snapped the barracks and Mike standing with his hands clasped behind him, his mouth sober, his eyes just visible under the stiff, black brim of his hat, trying to look like a marine poster. After an hour, his mom and dad had to catch the transport bus back to Los Angeles. His mother left him with four dozen cookies and the promise of as many as he could eat during his leave. His dad gripped Mike's hand so firmly that Mike could feel the pressure of the bones. His dad clasped his shoulder, letting his hand linger there, then cleared his throat and turned to his wife. They all smiled, and then his parents stepped up into a dull green bus, calling over their shoulders, "See you in four weeks."

Mike waved to his mom and then stiffly saluted his dad, holding the salute until the bus pulled away.

Within a day or two of graduation, everyone received orders. Mike opened his stiff envelope, tugged out the precisely typed sheet, then hesitated. Others seemed as excited and as reluctant. There were a few exaggerated moans; some wide grins. One guy muttered an oath, threw down his orders, and deliberately stomped on them, leaving a dusty boot tread; but then he bent and brushed off the sheet, tucking it gently into his breast pocket with his fingertips.

Mike opened his. Radio school. Nothing fancy, nothing flashy. Radio and Communications Operations. With no luck at all, he'd be among August replacements for Vietnam.

That same week the company was scheduled for their first liberty. They could check out and go anywhere within a hundred-mile radius as long as they were back in the barracks by midnight Sunday. Where to go? They talked about it in the barracks that night. Some couldn't wait to hit the round of bars, to find drinks and girls. Mike was reluctant to talk about where he wanted to go. But finally he found five or six others who wanted to go to Disneyland too.

Back at camp, after hot dogs and plastic dolls dressed in green feathers and Huck Finn's Island, they went on learning how to lob grenades and shoot bazookas and use flame throwers with some accuracy, even in the wind.

It rained and turned freezing cold. After boot camp's rigor, this routine seemed easy. Mike caught a light case of pneumonia and was in the rack for three days with a cough and a throat too sore to swallow. The corpsman gave him two shots, some chalky, pink-coated tablets to swallow, and stocked him up on nose drops, Kleenex, and medicated lozenges.

Mike tried to join Force Recon, a special unit, partly because he was disgusted with the lack of discipline, the sloppy un-marine attitude that had rooted in, and partly because he wanted to get away from the split developing in the company between those who frequented the barracks house up the hill filled with drinking and gambling by candle stub and those who didn't. Even the crisp uniforms they had worn so proudly at graduation seemed limp and dirty around the edges to Mike. He wanted the imposed discipline of Recon, but they took men only out of every other company, so Mike had to stay with radios, learning how to pack them, carry them, use them. He made a calendar on the back of one of the envelopes from home and checked off the days until leave. His family made his plane reservation and had to change it because the sergeant said the company would stay an extra day for review.

Finally, duffel bag in hand, he was walking across the asphalt to the airplane. He felt impressive, hard-muscled, dangerous, one khaki uniform on a plane full of business suits and severe ties.

At home Mike shed his uniform for old patched jeans and a torn T-shirt and went for the basketball court. Mom cooked his favorite foods, and he slept as late as he wanted, sprawled in pillows and tumbled quilts until the sun made bright patterns across his room. The little ones stayed up too late watching him clown around the kitchen, try to juggle popcorn, and play cards betting chocolate chip cookies. Steve kept telling him he should take out his English teacher, who was young and divorced and laughed easily with the students. Finally, she pulled up in front of their house one day in her flashy red convertible. She had given Steve a lift home from the junior high.

Mike was outside working over the lawn mower. He waved to Steve's hello, wiped his hands on a black rag, and sauntered across the lawn. She *was* pretty, dark hair held back in a bright scarf patterned in reds and golds, lips and fingernails frosted white. Mike hooked his thumb in his waistband and saw her eyes drop to his chest and shoulders. When she looked up, a little smile was on her lips.

At midnight, they were kissing in her car. Mike had never moved so fast, felt so free. Was it being a marine? He didn't call her again. He didn't want to think where another session in her car might end. When he got home that night, he saw that someone, his dad maybe, had cleaned up the lawn mower and put it away.

Sundays the entire family went to church. Mike sat alert, watching every detail, memorizing the sagging edges of the faces who had been his growing up. He watched the dust filtering through the sunshine, hovering over the bluish hair of a grandmother and the ringlets of the little girl beside her. The child watched Mike watch, her eyes big and one finger in her mouth.

A letter came, stiff on official yellow paper. His leave had been shortened by four days. And his assignment had been changed to machine guns.

His dad had marked and Lynn had cut out every article in the paper about Vietnam. Mike had put off reading the clippings. Now he read them. Afterwards he took his basketball and went to the court at Lynn's school. He twirled the ball on one forefinger, rolled it from fingertip to shoulder and back, dribbled the ball between and around his legs, pumped baskets, pounding the ball up and down the uneven pavement, swishing, ringing, catching the ball on the rebound and bouncing it back up into the hoop. He concentrated only on the movements—clean, hard, precise. When the kids came screaming out for lunch and kickball, he tucked the ball onto his hip and walked back home, lightly, easily.

3

Hotel Company

January 1967. During the flight back to Los Angeles Mike sat quietly, his mind behind a careful mental curtain, partitioned off and remote. He couldn't remember the color of the stewardess's hair or the name of the movie or what they had been served for meals, and he couldn't force his thoughts into patterns or words.

Then the airplane landed, and he walked down the rolled rubber treads of the sidewalk to the asphalt. He had seen the waiting truck with the driver leaning against the hood, smoking his cigarette. Two or three others were walking with him towards the truck. He didn't remember them from the airplane. Setting his own bag on the tailgate, he swung aboard. The others pushed in behind him, settling on the benches. One boy stretched out, propped his shoulders back, folded his arms across his chest, and dropped his chin down to the neck of his T-shirt. No one spoke.

Mike was the last one back to the hut. The others watched him go to his locker, spin it open, and unzip his bag. Renby, greasy playing cards still in his hands, moved over and leaned against Mike's bunk.

"You were squad leader, man. What's happening? Why we all back early?"

Mike shrugged. He could feel their pressuring silence. "I don't know, Rink, I don't know." Mike finished emptying his bag and shut the locker carefully. He knew they were still watching him. "My dad says there's been some heavy losses in 'Nam." He looked around. "I guess they need more bodies."

The silence finally broke that night. Propped up on elbows or legs dangling off the bunks, they smoked and argued. No one had read the newspapers about Vietnam, so they could only speculate and complain about the four days of leave.

The next morning jungle training started—a new company of guys, new leaders and sergeants. They went without water under the hot sun with flak jackets and heavy packs, slept little, and headed out in the California bush again. If they fell asleep, they'd be slapped awake and given extra patrols, extra watch. They learned to shoot the M-16s off their thighs and hips in silent simulated jungles where targets popped up suddenly behind bushes or trees. Points were tallied. If they missed the targets, eventually they "died." They went on scouting patrols and hunted each other down, staged a mock war with play land mines and booby traps but real bullets that hit the targets with sharp pings.

Mike was tired, but he thought it was fun. In the corner of his mind he knew this wasn't play, but he could slip through the bushes, shoot targets, and keep his points low, keep himself "alive." It was like stealing a basketball out of an opponent's hand and racing down court to a perfect lay-up.

While they sweated and shot and stalked and listened to others report on Vietnam, Mike deliberately kept that country in the distance. These were stories, and anyone could tell stories. Mike concentrated instead on little things: the feel of a smooth shot from his hip, the smell of the morning before the heat and the sun, the sounds of the bush, the letters in ink and pencil from home.

Soon there were only three or four days left—staging battalion. They had liberty all day and every night, and the officers in charge didn't care how late you came in or what you did as long as you made roll call each morning. They called out names, and soldiers who could barely stand called out "Yes, sir!", and then everyone would break for the gates again.

Mike went with his friend Steve Ware, whose parents lived in Los Angeles. They had a pool with slick blue tiles and wood decks and lemon-flowered plastic lounge chairs. They sat in wet bathing suits and drank fruit juice over ice, and Steve called some girls he knew.

Mike especially liked Connie. When she came out of the pool with her swimsuit clinging to her and her dark hair wet around the small gold earrings, Mike wanted to stay by the pool and never move.

Mike and Connie drove in her convertible to Las Vegas and danced all night. She wore white- and blue-flowered silk and a perfume that Mike could smell as they maneuvered through the crowded dance floors and leaned laughing on the bars for cold drinks. Mike laughed bubbles in his drink and into his nose until he coughed. They stayed too late and had to floor the accelerator to make it back for roll call.

As they drove, laughing at first and then tired, Mike could feel the shield around his fear cracking. The white sun on the sand seemed like a shell bursting. He wanted to turn the steering wheel and head away from the western sea.

"Tired?" She looked over and smiled.

"After last night? No way!" He made his voice breezy.

"If we don't get back, they may just boot you out."

He put his right hand onto her knees, across her hand. Her palm turned up to meet his, and he laced his fingers through hers. They decided she would wait while he checked in and then they would drive back to Steve's house.

Roll call started. Mike listened only for his own name. He thought about that morning on the freeway, not about Connie's mouth parting over her teeth or the blue eyeshadow in melted creases over her eyes, but about the fear he had felt.

"PFC Johnson, Mike."

"Yes, sir."

Connie came only to his shoulder, even in her high-heeled sandals. He liked being tall.

"Dismissed." Tonight they could swim until midnight in the cool water or head for the beach, the sand still warm.

"Johnson, hey, Johnson."

Rink and J. J. grabbed him.

"Man, you can't go. You got to check in. You're listed, posted, boy, on duty."

Mike grinned. "Oh, yeah. I know. But I can't keep a lady waiting." He turned to go, but J. J. grabbed him again.

"Hey, man, no joke. I'm serious."

Mike stood, blank, quiet. He could hear pounding in his head, like the surf pounding the beach, like guns pounding heat-baked earth.

He muttered an oath. "You can take this lousy place and its chain link fences and just shove it." He was shaking violently. He wanted to smash Rink's face.

Rink slid sideways a step. Mike brushed past, picked up his liberty pass, and headed for the waiting car.

The last night everyone stayed in the airport barracks and listened all night to the planes taking off and landing. It was May 30, 1967. There were long lines at the telephones. As he waited his turn, Mike bought a package of gum at the candy machine and chewed one stick after another. He talked to his mom and dad, swallowing against the tension. Mike didn't bother to unmake his bed that night. He drifted about with the others. Mike thought of Connie and skipping duty that last night. No one had said a thing. Had the guys covered for him somehow? Mike shrugged it off as a concern from another time.

The next morning two stewardesses were waiting for them on the steps of a Continental Airlines jet. There were at least six more waiting outside. "Give them ten stewardesses before they hit the bush, a blonde for every boy off to war." Mike almost smiled at the thought. He did smile at one of the girls, patting his knees to invite her to sit down next to him. She arched her eyebrows, winked as she refused, and asked if she could do anything else for him.

Even airline food tasted good after the mess hall. One soldier joked about a dying man's last request, "A good meal, a final cigarette, and a pretty woman." They all laughed at that one and kept repeating it. The laughing and joking eased their tension. Mike scribbled a note home. The stewardesses weren't the cutest but the chow was great. He was anxious to get started and get it over with. He'd been trained with the best and would be fighting with the best. The weather got a little rough, and he signed off, "Love you all a bunch."

They spent four days in Okinawa, withering in the heat, going to the PX, playing cards, and circulating stories about the awful diseases they would catch if they went off base. Mike spent most of his time in the swimming pool. Finally the order came, "Saddle up. We're going tonight."

The airport smelled of exhaust and burned rubber. While the marines stood in line, the officers huddled over the last of the paperwork. And then they were inside the plane—no padded seats or smiling stewardesses this time. The men sat facing each other across a wide aisle. Mike could see the metal tubing in the floor and sides. At 12:30 they took off. Without insulation, the four big engines pounded through the walls. But no one wanted to talk anyway.

It was early morning when the big jet entered Vietnamese airspace. Mike noticed the dust first, a faint red haze. The land inside the circles of barbed wire looked baked and brittle, like a brick left too long in the kiln. The violent green crowded against the fences and wound twisted fingers between the low hills. They circled Da Nang. The mountain thrust up from the center of the bay, with the old shanty tiers packed between the water and the land.

Mike stepped off the plane and was swallowed indifferently by the heat and the dust, though it was still early morning. He hadn't expected to scramble off under enemy fire, but he was surprised to just shoulder his duffel bag and walk into a building.

It wasn't any cooler inside. He went to the back of a long line of marines waiting by the tired letters of a sign labeled Processing. The military clerk inspected Mike's papers, stamped them in purple, and assigned him a tent without looking up.

Mike followed the stream of men to his tent. He dumped his duffel bag and hand satchel on the bed. Dust puffed up from the blankets. Mike spread a rip in the tent canvas at the head of his cot and looked out at the shimmering undulations of heat. He went to chow and had eggs and pancakes and cold milk, just like boot camp.

Outside, Vietnamese men and children held up trays of bright, papery things. Thin, nasal voices kept repeating, "Number one stuff. Number one stuff." The women with heavy black hair rolled up on their necks wore light, semifaded tunics over loose, black trousers. Mike's head ached with the noise and shouting, the steady pounding of planes, and the heat.

The tent was only a little quieter and no cooler. Finally he started writing. He wrote to anyone he could think of—to his uncle about the candy store, to Connie, his parents, his grandparents, to Lynn and Neal. He wrote until his fingers stiffened and he couldn't think of any more addresses. Then he discovered he had only one envelope. So he stuffed all of the letters but the one to his folks back in his bag.

The long afternoon finally deepened into blue. Just before

chow, an NCO stepped into the tent. "Outside." Mike and the others looked at each other as they unfolded from their cots and lined up outside.

"Smith, Second Battalion, First Marines; Jones, Third Battalion, Fourth Marines; Johnson, Second Battalion, Seventh Marine Regiment, First Division, 2-7 Hotel Company." Mike heard his name. There ought to be something more than this NCO with waxy shoes, he thought.

That night Mike lay on his cot and watched through the rip in the tent as the Phantoms blazed on the runway, kicked into first gear, and took off straight into the sky. They circled tight and high against the dark, sometimes lifting off in pairs and trios with only a few feet between their wings. Mike wondered how, with so many jets coming and going, they knew who came back. He imagined himself as a pilot, lifting out of the dirt and heat, rolling and turning against that mountain jutting from the bay. No little heat-stunted country could stop those beautiful jets.

In the morning Mike balanced his bag at the spot where the marines for the Second Battalion, Seventh Regiment would be picked up. Another soldier was already standing there, and two others followed Mike from his tent. One truck pulled through with the driver yelling, "Third Battalion, Third Battalion." He stopped the truck and swung open the door, stepping out onto the running board. He pulled two cigarettes out of his pocket and lit them both. His shirt was raggedly chopped off in back and had "Gook Killer" stenciled on it in black letters.

A new truck settled into the dust near Mike's group. Mike saw the polished M-16s before he noticed the ragged men who climbed out of the truck and motioned Mike's group inside. The floor of the truck was lined with sandbags. The truck reversed, pitching the men backwards. Mike wedged his feet between the bags and wished for a rifle.

The battalion was mounded and secured from the jungle with endless coils of barbed wire. A straw-and-mud village stood nearby. Mike caught a quick glimpse of a dog, and a woman bent over under a huge bundle. A bank of guns pointed into the sky from one side of the hill, and sandbags piled around holes pitted the rest of the mound.

The truck stopped in front of a large tent with screened walls and a tin roof. Inside two soldiers with old black typewriters sat at desks spread with paper. One marine stopped typing. Mike gave his name and orders.

Hotel Company 41

"Can you type?"

"Yes."

The marine put a finger in his ear. "How fast?"

"Pretty fast. I had some typing in high school and college."

"Come here." Mike followed him to an officer in the rear of the tent.

"Sir, this guy can type. Had typing in high school and college."

The officer put down his pen and opened Mike's folder, riffling through the pages.

"Son, you want to stay in battalion here and work as a clerk typist?"

Mike looked at him. "Sir?"

"We could use another typist in the office here."

Mike couldn't make the words make sense. All the sweat and training and work of boot camp, to be a marine, to shoot straight, to fight. To come to Vietnam and type? Not to carry a gun on patrol, not to watch for gooks?

Mike said firmly. "No sir. I'd like to go out in the field." Mike heard the typewriter nearby stop.

"Well, it's your life." The officer picked up his pen, wrote on Mike's file, and waved him on. The typewriter started its steady pinging again. "Hotel Company. They'll be in to get you."

At the supply issue room Mike got his flak jacket, extra boots, socks, dog tags with rubber edges so they wouldn't jingle, jungle fatigues, dark green T-shirts and shorts, a belt with a couple of canteens, a pack, and finally the M-16. Mike sighted down the rifle. He felt back in control again.

Just after chow the next evening, a gunnery sergeant came looking for Mike.

"Johnson, you got guard duty, hole five by the wire. Be out there pronto."

Mike picked up his rifle and clips. He checked out his equipment and then went down the hill in the twilight, looking for the hole. He could hear water running and dishes clinking as the last Vietnamese still inside the camp cleaned up the mess hall.

Sandbags surrounded the hole. Four-by-fours propped in the hole held up a square roof covered with more sandbags. The other marine on guard duty was already there, his air mattress spread on top of the sandbag roof, his rifle propped between his knees. He was whistling softly.

Posing with M-16 for a picture to send home

Mike (center) in front of tent shared with
10–12 other marines

"You Johnson?"
"Yeah."
"Stateside?"
"Three days ago."
"Mitchell." He whistled again. "I'm beat. How about taking first watch?"

Mike spread out his air mattress, wondering if they should be in the hole. He remembered stories about the Viet Cong, how they greased their bodies and wore only black loincloths and slipped through three rows of tangled wire to drop grenades into holes and slit the throats of sleeping soldiers. Mike studied the wire, the barbed layers tangled like steel tumbleweed. He fingered his gun.

"What are the cans for?"

Mitchell was spreading out his poncho. "Hang those empty puppies on the wire, put pebbles in them, man, and if anything touches that wire, you hear it." He stopped, soundlessly sucking his whistle against his teeth. "Sometimes the sound don't mean nothing, but you always hear it." He pulled his poncho over his head in heavy folds and stretched out, holding his rifle. "Can't none of them gooks get through without noise." He pulled his helmet down over his nose.

Mike could see the outlines of the village roofs against the jungle. The guards were herding the last Vietnamese workers outside the barbed wire, pulling the wire up and closing the gates. A few dim, smoky fires burned in the village. Mike shivered and put on his utility jacket, careful that the folds didn't get tangled with his rifle. Near the mountains a white light burst, small and bright. After a second Mike saw another flash and heard the artillery.

This is real, he thought. He swallowed and brought his finger nearer to the trigger of his M-16. Mitchell was breathing softly into his helmet. As the air cooled, a heavy dampness settled, and the mosquitoes came swarming out. They made Mike's nose itch, but he was afraid to scratch because he thought he might miss something in the dark. He strained at each sound, rehearsing boot-camp practice in his mind. Four pop flares. He brushed the mosquitoes away swiftly with his left hand and gripped the rifle again.

The wire rattled. He jerked his rifle up. He held it there stiffly, turning from side to side. Two or three mosquitoes whined about his face, and he felt them settle. Finally Mike slapped them and then silently prayed, "Dear God, don't let me be shot." He remembered nightmares from his childhood that left him screaming and wetting the bed.

Mitchell grunted and rolled onto one side. Mike saw two red flares now and remembered the orders, "Fire a red if you're hit or if you're being hit." He could feel the sweat collecting under his jacket and tasted salt on his upper lip. What was the sound across the wire? He realized that his jaw ached from clenching his teeth. He forced himself to take a long breath through his mouth. His tongue tasted coppery. Red flares. The rumble of artillery was consistent now. He had blocked out everything but the wire. How long? he wondered.

Mitchell took second watch, and Mike pretended to sleep, his eyes wide open inside of his helmet. But Mitchell seemed undisturbed, whistling softly.

They switched watch again, and again. Mike never did sleep. Finally the sky lightened a shade, and the artillery trailed off. A woman came out of one of the huts and started a small fire. Mike could hear birds. The gates opened, and finally they checked off guard duty for chow.

Mike and four others were driven twenty miles further west to Hotel Company. Hotel Company was a hill with artillery near the base, screened in barbed wire, tents at the end of the dusty road which wound to the top.

Mike was assigned to squad leader Corporal Barnes. Mike followed this tall, heavy-set man with the hard shoulders and thought he looked like he belonged there. Sandbags were piled three deep around the tent. Both ends of the tent were open to the afternoon. A group lounged around two cots which had been covered with a board to make a card table. Barnes pointed to a cot. A couple of men glanced up from the card game, but no one really said hello.

"That's Anderson, Lopez, Smither, Mack. Find your way around. We've got patrol tonight, so hustle through chow."

Mike arranged his things around the cot. The hill looked over the surrounding jungle, green waves that rolled back as far as Mike could see. Here and there were large open patches of diked-off rice paddies glistening silver in the sun. Mike scouted over the tents, talked to a few people, ate, but he couldn't stop looking out into that impenetrable green washing around their hill.

About ten men were going on patrol. Mike joined them, rubbing soft green camouflage over his forehead, cheekbones, and down into the neck of his green T-shirt. He was to carry the radio. The forty-pound backpack pulled up the edge of his flak jacket. Most of the others weren't wearing their jackets, but the metal links gave Mike a feeling of heavy comfort.

They started down the hill. Mike coiled the headpiece about his collar so he could still hear command as they talked softly. Barnes led them out of the gate then dropped back near the radio, and the point man struck out. Mike tried to avoid loose rocks, which turned noisily under his feet.

Just before they reached the black jungle edge, the radio headphone crackled softly by his ear. "Hotel One, Hotel One, how do you copy, over?" Mike silently keyed the answer with his handset. Then he was in the silent blackness under the trees, straining to see Barnes. He tried to shift the radio without clicking his flak jacket.

They passed a village of woven, untidy huts with barbed wire thrown up in jagged circles. Two water buffaloes were staked horns down near a hut within the circle. It was so quiet that Mike could hear chickens settling in with sleepy clucks. More than one baby was crying.

Mike jumped when the radio spoke again in his ear. He keyed twice, the signal that all was okay. Ahead Mike could see dark figures climbing onto the dikes between the rice paddies. He stepped off the firm road onto the soft dirt of the dike and had to hurry to keep up. His foot slipped on the soft edge, and he splashed, sinking to his hip in the heavy clay and water. Instantly the patrol was flat against the dike, guns ready.

"You dumb . . ." someone hissed. Mike measured the cold silence. He pulled his foot out of the sucking mud and stepped on the dike, awkwardly shifting the radio. Doing something stupid could mean their lives; Mike knew that. It was unforgivable in this group of men who had only the night's work to hold them together.

Mike fell twice more on the dike. He was soaked, and furious at having to carry the radio. They went into the jungle, leaving the rice paddies liquid-quiet behind them. Mike's boots squished softly. The anger helped his head clear. They moved through the grass and trees, drawing ever-wider circles.

Occasionally Mike saw the dull gleam of metal, but mostly he just followed his anger, souring with the dawn into self-disgust.

All night Mike had keyed okay, okay, no action. They lit off flares to signal they were coming in, no trouble.

"You did okay. You'll get used to it." Barnes had come over as Mike was unloading the radio and pistol.

The second night on patrol Mike left his flak jacket behind. The third night he left his helmet. They alternated patrol with guard duty. Soon he didn't notice the coppery taste in his mouth, and he started to sleep when he wasn't on watch.

His family sent a box with candy and socks. He wrote home asking for camera and film and adhesive tape for the countless nicks and cuts from the undergrowth.

Mike's patrol was sent back to a spot where another patrol had been ambushed. The jungle trail paralleled the base of a hill along a flat stream and an open area of grass. The VC had sat on the hill and shot the bellies out of nearly an entire patrol coming up the road. The eight men in Mike's patrol walked down that same road now, tense and quiet. The only Vietnamese Mike had seen were the ones from the village who worked in camp, and they were always locked out at night.

Mike's lips were dry, and he darted his tongue lightly over them. He fingered the action of his rifle. The closer to the hill, the faster his finger moved. Mike had learned not to focus and strain to see in the dark. When you let the dark and the sounds and the smells drift in, you could sense those strange, frail hints which could save your life.

They skirted around the end of the hill, hiked to the top, and dropped back down the hillside as quietly as possible to set up behind some bushes. For some reason no one dug in. Mike couldn't sleep. He checked the magazine in his rifle again. Tomorrow he would write home that they were winning the war, beating the enemy. He might kill a man tonight. From ambush it should be easier than shooting a deer. Mike waited and watched all night. Nothing happened. He was relieved. He was disappointed. He was still waiting for the test of all that training.

At four in the morning the patrol leader roused the only man sleeping and moved them back up the hill and down to the road. Mike thought of the man behind the desk, waving a coffee cup and asking Mike if he wanted to type. He lined up in the mess tent for breakfast, then dropped onto the cot for two or three hours before he was called out into the jungle again.

Two nights later the Viet Cong slipped like greased shadows into the village at the foot of the hill and sprayed the village chief's hut with a shower of lead. The guards on duty heard the noise and woke the entire company, but Charlie was long gone, leaving only the contemptuous bloody hut.

A big operation up into Happy Valley (a Viet Cong stronghold) was postponed so the company could guard the village, protect the villagers, and get another chief elected. Mike spent one day in the dusty perimeter of the village watching the slow election, the old men sitting in a circle while the women carried water or cooked rice over small fires. The older people ignored the marines, but the children came, shyly teasing for gum and offering dirty souvenirs.

Mike watched them, wondering what it would be like to live in this hot, straw-enclosed, barbed-wire place. He thought about his parents and their comfortable, slightly shabby furniture, how the house always seemed to smell of something good —like fresh bread. It seemed a long time since he'd smelled a good smell. None of the babies here wore diapers. Nearly everybody just went where the mood moved them. He wrinkled his nose.

With all the waiting, Mike asked for permission to go into battalion to see a dentist. A filling had come loose. It didn't hurt, but he could feel the hole fill up with soggy C rations when he ate. He caught a ride with a supply-and-mail truck. The driver talked about how many times his truck had been shot at and how he'd just kept driving. Occasionally they passed a child perched on a water buffalo or a woman balancing a huge load on her rusty bicycle.

"Got any souvenirs?"

"No, not yet." Mike coughed as dirt rolled in. "I'm going to send some stuff home to my family, though—a machete maybe. Took a few pictures."

The driver was shaking his head. "No, I mean gook souvenirs—belt buckles or shells or something. I got me this buddy who's got a collection. He got him a helmet and a belt buckle and a couple of little pin things and a knife."

Mike wondered how the friend got close enough to get the knife. They swerved past a group of people on foot. The old man had a mattress rolled on his back and pots hanging from it.

"Lousy strays." The driver laughed and slapped the wheel. "You know the best thing this guy's got?"

Mike shook his head.

"Man, he's got three ears." The driver grinned. "Now I'm not sure where he got them, but if I know Compton . . ."

Mike folded his arms over his chest and looked out of the window. He felt like he'd just been kicked in the stomach. You didn't even do that to a deer.

Mike went to the PX and paid an outrageous sum for a bottle of 7-Up, then on to the dentist. The slim, white-coated dentist had a light touch in Mike's mouth. He packed the tooth full, smoothed it, and gave it a last polish with a piece of gauze in a thin clamp.

Mike wandered over to the PX, flipping idly through their limited magazines and trying to remember if he needed more envelopes. He stopped in front of the shoelaces and polish and razors and soap, absently running his finger across his chin. Should he get more soap? He had just written home to please send socks, good white ones dyed dark green, and Lifebuoy; this soap looked like the grainy kind that went gray and didn't lather. He bought a postcard to send Barbara because her last letter had promised chocolate-chip cookies. Mail had been real good, Mike thought. A steady stream of letters from home and Barbara and Lynn and a couple of packages. He took the last stick of gum from the package out of his pocket, unwrapped it, and bent it into his mouth. The mint flavor rushed up his tongue. Mike crumpled the tin foil and popped it like a mini-basketball past the corner of the counter.

Then he wandered back out of the PX, glad to be idle, his hands in his pockets and almost sleepy in the sun. Steve Ware was somewhere around here. He'd relayed a message up the line to Mike that he was in battalion filing papers, and how was the front line? Mike found the big building piled with sandbags and covered with tin. Inside he could see Steve, his back to the door, rapidly sorting a sheaf of papers into files. The files had rusty, beaten-in sides and sat lopsided. Steve slammed the drawer. It was crooked, and he yanked it back out to shove it in again.

Mike grinned. "All this is in the line of duty?"

Steve jerked around. "Mike!" and they were half-tussling, half-hugging each other and pounding each other on the back.

Hotel Company

"Hey, let me see if I can get off and we'll go get a soda. What you here for anyway?"

Mike tapped his cheek. "Lost a filling 'bout a week and a half ago. No real action, so I came in to have it filled up again."

"Teeth chattering too hard, are they?" Steve laughed, then abruptly sobered. "I thought I'd wet my pants the first night on guard duty."

Mike nodded. "Yeah, I know."

"Well, hey, just a minute."

They went back to the PX and settled down over a soft drink.

"How's it out there?" Steve looked up at Mike carefully, quizzically; and Mike all of a sudden felt awkward about his being there and Steve being in here, in battalion, secure with men and artillery and permanence.

"Oh, it's just . . . well, you know." Mike shrugged. "Hot, scary at night. We run patrols and stuff in the day."

Steve looked him over. "How'd you get so beat up?" and Mike realized he was noting all the bandages, cuts, and infected bites that you just couldn't keep clean and dry and uninfected. Mike shrugged. "Just out on patrol. Grass cuts are the worst."

Steve was silent for a moment. "Shot anyone yet?"

"No."

Steve concentrated on his drink. Mike looked at him and then away, and looked at Steve again. "Naw. The closest I got was when they blew up the village."

Mike tried to down the last of his soda in one breath. He found a truck headed back out and rode on the sandbags.

That night Mike was assigned radio for patrol under Corporal Parker, the black squad leader. Two squads were to go out and run ambush, one to the west and the other to the east. Mike watched the two squad leaders talking as he rubbed the camouflage over his face and checked his rifle. They packed up and marched down the hill and out through the barbed wire. But the two squads didn't separate. They tramped softly along the road for about two-hundred yards. Then the two leaders stopped and eased the men off into the grass.

Parker, the squad leader, was holding his rifle down. "I don't think we'll run ambush tonight. We'll just stay here where the enemy won't be walking and rest." The two leaders glanced at each other across the darkening air. "Lie in a circle with your feet in, your head and rifle out. Every other one will sleep.

Then we'll trade off. Any questions?" The marines humping the radios shifted uneasily. "Oh yeah. Every half-hour radio check, just answer ambush site, something like that." He shifted his gun and pointed around the circle. "You sleep, you watch. Sleep. Watch."

Mike lay down with the rest of them in a circle. The jungle grass reached up over his head, blacking out the hill. He felt odd. The acid feeling of disappointment was back, deflated anticipation, and relief he didn't want to acknowledge. Finally he shrugged and rolled over to sleep. Somebody nudged him awake for the eleven-to-one watch. Mike sat up, a little cold and stiff, hunching and straightening his shoulders to ease the muscles. Quickly the men who had been watching stretched out, their rifles close by their sides, and fell asleep. At eleven-thirty the radio crackled softly, and Mike picked up the headphone. He keyed twice that all was secure. The radio puttered softly and went still. Mike sat, hunched over, cross-legged, his rifle across his lap, watching the dark hill in front of him. The radio called in at midnight; one of the other marines keyed back.

"Johnson?" The whisper came soft.

"Yeah."

"What do you think they'd do if they caught us?"

Mike opened his mouth to answer but was interrupted by two sharp cracks of ground fire. Rounds of bullets poured in at the hill, burning through the broken silence.

Mike slapped a magazine into his rifle and snapped into position prone. The radio was crackling, "Position! What's your position?" The black man kicked Mike. "Don't shoot. They don't know we're here, and they'll blow us apart."

"Hotel one, where are you? What are your coordinates?" The black corporal circled frantically. "Get down. Shut up. Don't shoot. Nobody shoot or I'll kick your butt." He grabbed the radio.

"Position." He fired off a set of coordinates, somewhere close to the place they were supposed to be. Mike was quivering over his gun, but his locked arm was rock steady. The hill was so bright he could see the gunnery sergeant running from bunker to bunker with a pistol in his hand, could almost hear individual words. His finger was locked on the trigger. The man next to him was cursing in a soft, fluid, breathless tone Mike could barely hear. Mike flattened closer into the grass. He could hear the VC in the weeds, shadowy figures rustling by, funneling steadily towards the hill.

The hill exploded again, tanks going up in lazy pieces. Something blew apart in the air overhead, and the world flooded with white light. "Watch the canisters, watch the canisters." Battalion was shooting huge flares over the hill and surrounding area to light everything up. The hollow canisters fell off, leaving the flares drifting under parachutes. The hundred-pound canisters landed with dull thuds in the grass and bushes, one just twelve feet from where the ambush lay.

The firing eased a little. Then from half a mile behind them, about where the ambush should have been, the rockets started firing. They were rocketing battalion and miles past that to Da Nang, with no one to blow them out of position. Battalion fired artillery shells back, throwing dirt into the sky. The hill fired aimlessly, fruitlessly. Battalion finally got a fix on the position and started firing with deadly accuracy, but it was now getting late. The sky behind the hill was graying toward day.

Mike uncurled a little, the clench of terror deep inside easing. No one had found them. Mike could now see the man next to him. A heavy hum started in from the east, getting louder. Mike squinted against the sky.

"Here comes Puff." A ponderous old airplane slowly droned its way in, its propellers blurring, guns blasting from every angle.

"Good old Puff." The man next to Mike was watching too.

"How come you can see the firing lines?" Mike was amazed.

"Every fifth bullet's a tracer. Phosphorus on it. When it hits the air, it burns." The marine reached in his front pocket for gum, the words slipping out as relief from the night. "Puff puts out so much it's like a solid line of bullets; tons and tons. Penetration power absolute. That sweetie can cover every foot of a football field with bullets in just seconds." They watched the plane sweep the area where the rockets had come from.

"Okay. Move!" The corporal was on his feet, dusting off his rifle, yanking the radio up on his back. "Move! We've got to get in without the hill seeing us, or they'll shoot."

The marines skirted the side of the hill, bent over into the grass and bushes. They came in on the road, sending up two flares to notify the hill that all was okay.

The Viet Cong had just walked in the gate. They had walked up in marine flak jackets and helmets. They said, "Patrol coming in," and the guards at the gate let them in. No one fired a shot. One guard kept swearing. "It was perfect English, perfect English." Only later did they find one of the guards at the gate lying in his own blood, his throat slit.

Once inside they had broken into silent groups. One threw satchels filled with plastic explosives, nails, and glass on the motor and electric works of the artillery so that even if the explosion was small, the guns wouldn't work. They blew up the tanks and tossed grenades into a tent where two marines were sleeping. They stripped to black loincloths and greased skin to slip out through the barbed wire. The gunnery sergeant had shot one of them in the back of the head with his pistol.

Three marines had been killed. Mike was assigned to go down to artillery and bring the bodies up so they could be shipped home. One man's chest was blown open. The marine who had been killed at the gate looked bloodless, chalky white. Mike helped pick them up and carry them to the jeep. They were already stiff.

Mike held them on the truck. When the jeep stopped, he carried their feet while another soldier picked up their shoulders. Mike eased each foot cautiously onto the dust, knowing that it made no difference how gentle he was. He kept looking at them even after the driver had wrapped each in his poncho.

Later someone tied the dead Vietnamese soldier to the back of a utility truck by the right foot and drove all around the camp. Mike unlocked his duffel bag and took some pictures of the body dragging behind the truck. That was the only one of the enemy he had seen, and he wanted the picture to make it real.

When Mike saw anyone from the ambush, they would question each other with their eyes. But no one found out. Two squads went out to find where the VC had launched the rockets. They found indentations in the ground not far from where Mike figured they should have run ambush that night. He looked at the holes, wondering if they could have stopped the attack or if they would have been killed. The damage report said supply fifteen miles away was leveled, Kilo Company and India Company were damaged, battalion hit.

Mike played poker, feeling a little guilty after being brought up so strictly. He lost six dollars and then won back seventy-five to send home. He still humped the radio on patrol and night ambush, and the fact that he hadn't been shot at or shot at anything kept winding him up tighter and tighter inside. The brass warned the squads that at the end of the month they'd be sent on a week-long operation up into Happy Valley.

Parker was fidgeting and blinking when he announced it, lower lip loose and wet. "You'll carry the radio, Johnson," he said, not really looking at Mike, but menacing anyway.

"All right," Mike shrugged.

"Man, you'll say all right." Parker didn't have a T-shirt on and his body shone with sweat. "You don't know nothing, kid."

Everybody stiffened just slightly. Parker had been out about ten months and he was good, but he was skating, eating up time safely by avoiding patrols, going into battalion to have his eyes examined or his teeth checked. Mike had watched him in the bush and wondered if he himself would be jumpy when he had been there a year. They'd already had a couple of minor tussles because Mike had suspected, then finally caught him looking through Mike's duffel bag.

"Johnson." He picked up his rifle in one powerful hand, balancing and pointing it across at Mike, his face gleaming and set. "I'm going to kill you next time you go out. You don't know nothin'." Mike could feel the sweat between his shoulder blades. He said nothing, just stared coldly at the big marine. Parker turned away and put down the rifle.

The days settled into an endless round of patrols and ambushes, night watch and patrols. Mike didn't go out with the black corporal again. He stopped carrying the radio and started walking point, lead man, because his eyes were sharp and his reflexes were excellent.

During one watch the VC hit again, trying to blow up a giant helicopter that landed on the hill, its fuel lines damaged by ground fire, but they didn't get it. The patrol rode guard on a truck convoy, bouncing on the hard sandbags until their tailbones were sore.

One afternoon some of them were up on the hill by the company officers' tent, where someone had strung a volleyball net between two tents. Mike enjoyed the knot and flow of leaping up for a spike, catching a powerful overhand serve with the thrust of his thumbs wedged together so it popped back over the net. He was hardly aware of the artillery firing support for one of the patrols. His side was winning, even

Mike and members of his squad, October 1967

though it was an easy game, not a hard battle for points. A line of clouds, dark and heavy, came in fast and the artillery had to stop firing because the electricity in the air could burst a shell as soon as it left the gun. When the artillery support stopped, the guns' regular boom dying before the thunder's threatening rumble, the marine serving hesitated. A patrol out there needed support and didn't have it now. He tossed up the ball and served, his fist slamming the ball into the net, losing the serve. They played until the rains swept in.

4

Point Man

Mike wrote home asking his dad to sharpen his buck knife and send it along with a sharpening stone, oil, and steel wool so he could keep it clean. He won a little more at cards. When cookies came, he shared them around the squad.

One night in late August, Mike's patrol went out and somehow wandered into the nearby South Vietnamese village. One of the soldiers who knew some Vietnamese knocked on the gate and talked with the sentries for a few minutes. The sentries turned the gate and waved the patrol in through the tangle of barbed wire.

There were one or two houses built of some brick with wood and odd bits of tin nailed up, but mostly they were dry grass and bamboo woven together, melded into shape with mud and rustling with insects. The guards carefully pulled the barbed-wire gates shut behind them; inside it felt almost like a carnival. They were laughing and joking, as though the only shooting was in a gallery at pop-down ducks, secure behind the barbed wire—cheap wire but still wire—instead of out in the dark jungle. Funny how the coils of barbed wire could close the constant shadows out of your head, leave you feeling free enough to joke and smile and relax your fingers around your gun.

Mike could hear low voices behind the thin walls, a mother hushing a baby. The smell of smoke from fires and of dust stirred up by their feet drifted together in a blue haze. The only light came from the red coals under cooking pots in front of the houses they passed.

They finally stopped in a two-room hut with three windows, built partially of cinder block, big enough to hold all eight of them. They dropped their packs to make backrests. One marine took a tiny packet out of his breast pocket, tapped it lightly against his palm, and then lifted it to his mouth. A soft tune wafted from his corner, like the shy smile of a new friend.

"The bear went over the mountain, the bear went over the mountain." The marine next to Mike softly mouthed the words while he hunted for matches. No one ever smoked on patrol. You could smell a cigarette a hundred yards away.

An old man shuffled into the room with a box. "Coke? You buy Coke?"

Mike unbuttoned his back pocket and brought out his military scrip, which could be traded for Vietnamese money. Someone else bought one. After lingering hopefully, the old man shuffled out of the hut.

The Coke tasted metallic, almost rusty, but it was wet, and American in the shape of the bottle and in the tall white letters curved around the side. Mike drank some, then got up, tucking his rifle under his arm, and wandered around the corner of the hut.

Off to the north he could see the liquid gleam of quiet rice paddies and the darker shape of water buffaloes. It was black enough that Mike knew no one could see him. But he unconsciously eased away from the cover of the huts, continuing his vague patrol. Finally he came back to the central building. Almost everyone was asleep. Mike laid down his pack and his radio and felt sleep falling as heavily as night. Later, Mike vaguely realized that the watch had changed.

The shots and flares brought rifles alert before the men were even awake. "Stay quiet until you see someone."

The watch at the door and windows hid carefully in the shadows where they could see without being outlined by the light from flares and burning huts.

"They're wiping out the village!"

"Marines, marines, marines." The Coke man screamed across the open spaces, then ran sobbing to the door, shooting a Browning automatic rifle at the flames. He wanted someone to follow him. Mike grabbed his pack. One other marine, Mollenpah, was behind Mike. The shooting was constant.

First the old man ran to the garbage area and began riddling an old barrel over and over, hysterically. Mike finally pulled the rifle from his hands. The drum was blown apart, but there was no body. They could see no one, nothing, so they ran back to the old man, following him in a maze through the huts. Everywhere was fire and blood. Finally they came to the other side of the village by the rice paddies. There the cut wire was pulled open as wide as a gate.

They had lost the old man now. Dimly, Mike realized that the two of them were alone. Mike saw a man lying in a pool of blood between two huts. A dog was licking his wrist. Only a piece of thumb bone and skin held the hand to his wrist. Mike could see the holes in his stomach and chest. He was mumbling.

"Mollenpah, cover me." Mike knelt in the blood, dropping his gun and tearing open his pack. He bandaged the wrist, heavily, hastily, then laid the compress on the man's chest. Mike ran back to the brick house for more compresses, shooting off to the right where the South Vietnamese were pointing as he ran. He ran back and kept bandaging the dying man. The dog stopped whining and wandered off. The alley seemed oddly quiet in the midst of the burning village. Mike bandaged every hole in the man.

"You'll be okay. Everything will be all right." Mike knew the man was past pain now, but the thought flashed through his mind as to whether someone should shoot him in the head, help him die. They left him lying in the alley and headed back to the rest of the patrol. Mike could see figures off to the right, running up the hill. He stopped, flung up the M-16, burning the hill with all the ammo he had. He couldn't see if he hit anyone. In three crazy minutes he unloaded two hundred rounds. Mike ran toward the brick building for more. They grabbed him as he came through the door.

"Man, we got to get gone."

Mike stopped cold. The hill didn't know they were here. They must call in support. The patrol set off cautiously, strung closely between the squad leader and Mike, who brought up the rear. They slipped across the road and then moved up a hill into some dense cover where they could look down on the burning village.

Three of them crawled under a poncho with a flashlight and a map to determine where they were and where they should be. Mike had the radio. He was afraid his voice would shake, but he radioed in, his voice controlled: "Hotel One, this is Hotel Six, over." Mike gave their coordinates and called in the artillery.

When he wound off, Mike could see that the squad leader was staring at him. "How we gonna explain all the empty shells in the compound? Why didn't you just leave a calling card saying 'marines were here'? And how would we have explained if you'd gotten your head shot off?"

"But that old man—he needed help. We were there . . ."

"We were not there. Do you understand? We were not there. Pull another stunt like that and I'm gonna cut off your ears and string them on barbed wire."

Mike realized the squad leader was as scared as he was.

Back in the tents no one said much. Lopez, another squad leader who shared the tent, finally broke off the stiff silence. He sat on the edge of his cot, paring his nails with a knife. "That was a dumb thing Johnson did." Mike kept his head down. "But I'd want him on my squad." Mike looked up and met Lopez's dark eyes. They measured each other for a long moment. Then Lopez's knife returned to its gentle paring.

After that, Mike started walking point more often, lead man.

In September the monsoons settled in. Rain came in continuous sheets except for an hour or two in the afternoon. The rice paddies filled up and spilled over the dikes. The jungle dripped and decayed. Periodically typhoons would come roaring in off the Gulf of Tonkin and dump sheets of ocean spray on the marines. The red dust turned to deep slippery mud.

Neither the men nor their gear were ever dry now. Mike was continually polishing, rubbing down, and cleaning his rifle to keep out the rust. Everything in the tent soured with mildew and started to look faintly green.

At times the sun did come out, and then the jungle became a steaming, sticky sauna. The warm wetness rose from the ground in an eerie mist. Leaves and grass stuck to the boots and clothes of the marines as they slogged through the dense jungle growth. Three hours patrol, three hours off. Sleep was a joke. Their skin wrinkled, folded, split, and peeled. Mike developed sores on his feet. The elephant grass, taller than a man, cut, and every cut gathered infection, bred it in the continuous damp.

One evening Mike reached his tent exhausted but determined to write a letter home. He entered his six-by-ten area, hung up his rifle, dumped water out of his helmet, hung up his flak jacket to drain, and completely stripped. He wiped himself down with a soggy towel and remembered taking a warm, fluffy, sweet-smelling towel out of the dryer after a shower at home. He groped through his duffel bag for anything even remotely dry, gave up, and pulled on a damp-green T-shirt and pants. Then he found his notepad:

Dear Family,

Hey! What's this Dad said about not having received any of my money? My bonds should still be in the Treasury Department—I think. I guess they are holding them for me. Write San Diego and ask—OK? I have sent checks home the first of September and October. Didn't you even get them? One was for $80—October, and another one was for about $64 (I think)—September. I'll send December's home so you can get presents.

I got a letter from Lloyd and Yvonne and Kathy and a bunch of people at church. Yes, I got Boyd's package, but I didn't know it was from him—I'll write and thank him. Our area is not quite as secure as our last area, but we've got a couple of armored amphibious tractors (amtracs) with 50 cal. machine guns to help out.

Well, guess who made Lance Corporal?—me!! As of October 1st, I'm L/Cpl.!!! My December and November checks will be $20 bigger! Might even be fire team leader pretty soon.

Congratulations to my star quarterback brother! You will really tear them up next year. Did everyone get to see you play? Next year maybe your big brother will get to see a few games. Maybe Miss Ferrell will go with me—why don't you ask her? (ha-ha).

You just can't believe how wet it is here. I am always wet, sometimes just soaked for hours. There is just no way to get dry. I feel like a walking prune I'm so wrinkled. By the way, if you could send me any rain gear, socks, boots—anything to help me keep dry, sure would appreciate it.

Well, I've gotta go on an ambush tonight—it only goes out 10,000 meters. Oh well, just nine more months.

      Love & miss ya all,
      Mike

And so the rainy season went: he never dared to wear underwear because of the possibility of jock itch; he had sore feet from soft, spongy, soggy skin; and constant skin infections necessitated constant antibiotics. It was a miserable time.

The wet days settled into a monotonous routine. The first stop in the morning was the chow tent with its door designed for Vietnamese, not six-foot-two West Virginians. Steam and smoke shrouded the cooks, who threw a couple of eggs and maybe some sausage on a plate. Mike then dipped into the community can for ketchup, worked the salt shaker over to break up the lumps, and ate. Then day patrol. The marines checked the villages, and the villagers were expected to come out and ask for help if they needed it. At seven or eight in the evening, the men prepared for night patrol, smearing their faces with green, making sure metal equipment didn't clink. They always took ponchos. Then it was decision time—who would carry the radio, who would fire automatic, semi-automatic, who would carry the M-79 grenade launcher, who would walk point, walk tail.

They found their spot, set up ambush, and took turns sleeping for two hours and standing guard for one hour. During an alert, they could sleep only a half-hour at a time, and during trouble everyone was up. Up and down. At five or so in the morning, before light, the patrol popped up flares and came back in. At the gate, guards carefully scrutinized the group as they announced, "Patrol coming in." The men got about three hours' sleep and then were at it again. Day after day. Week after week.

But time together didn't mean friendships. This war kept the men apart emotionally. They came in, eighteen- or nineteen-year-old rookies. Wetness, tension, erratic sleep patterns, uncertainty about that night or the next morning—men's nerves were raw, and they kept to themselves. Only the squad leaders stuck pretty much together. They knew what was going on. As the rookies became veterans during their twelve months in Vietnam, they also became cautious. They didn't want to lead or take responsibility for others. It was time to keep your tail down, play it safe, make it home. The seasoned veterans were either home or dead.

Mike found himself the favored point man. Out in front he hummed Christmas carols or licked at powdered chocolate drink he got in trade for the cigarettes he was issued but didn't use. Walking yards in front of the patrol was lonely, but Mike liked to feel dependent on himself and not on someone who didn't know what he was doing. Mike learned where to walk and where to expect trouble. As he approached a small valley between two hills, he knew what to look for. "No good. Doesn't feel right. Good place for a trap." He would take the men off over one of the hills, an unlikely place for an American patrol, or off the trail and into the jungle. He learned to stay off trails. Though daytime action was scarce, booby traps killed marines constantly.

In mid-October, Mike's patrol was sent to clean out an area where two marines had been killed by grenades dropped from a small cliff. Mike couldn't get those marines out of his mind. No chocolate powder and no singing on point this day. Mike had overheard the lieutenant arrange for artillery and F-4 Phantom coverage. Now he could see the small Cherokee buzzing in circles overhead, spotting for the patrol.

For two days the marines rambled through the hilly jungle but found nothing. The second night the patrol dug in on a hill. Mike had been aching, feeling dizzy all afternoon. He spent a restless night and in the heat of the next afternoon collapsed on the way back to his tent, rolling several feet down the hill.

"Hey, Johnson's down." Mike felt hands tugging at him, carrying him up the hill. His brain was swirling in confusion, and his stomach rolled its juices into his esophagus. He swallowed hard.

By the time they got him back to battalion, Mike was shivering constantly, his teeth chattering.

"Johnson, you goldbrick." It was Barnes. "You'll do anything to get out of a little walking. Now who do I put on point? You're the only bloodhound I've got!"

Mike managed a feeble smile at the corporal, then pulled the poncho closer toward him. His body crawled with icy sensations, felt bitter cold, and he couldn't stop his teeth from chattering. Mike's only consistent feeling was a weak ache.

A four-wheel drive "mule" took Mike to the battalion. Then the "duck," a tracked amphibious vehicle with 50-caliber machine guns, took him to the medical station, where a corpsman and then a military doctor examined him.

The next hours were a haze. He vaguely remembered a corpsman holding him naked under a cold shower, making him get up at night and walk.

"Leave me alone, man."

"Sorry, marine, we have to keep your temperature down. You don't have any extra brain cells. I'm doing you a favor, man."

Mike was transferred to Da Nang Military Hospital. They took his rifle away. That bothered him worse than hearing "malaria." Then the dreams began: train boxcars marked with big white X's; Uncle Boyd's candy store with rows of jaw breakers and multi-colored suckers; Yaz of the Red Sox belting a homer in the World Series; he and his father and grandfather working the hedges and tall grasses of the West Virginia woods, flushing the squirrels and birds—Mike smelled the sharp freshness in the autumn woods. Then the vomiting brought him back to foggy consciousness. He was still in 'Nam.

The days stretched into weeks of fans, alcohol baths, ice-water baths, blankets, nausea, headaches, medicine, boredom, and sleep. The finger pricks for blood samples drove him crazy.

"Oh, no, no more please."

"You know this is necessary, Johnson. The pathogens are most active in your bloodstream when you are running a high fever, which you are now. We suspect falciparum malaria, but we have to be sure."

One afternoon Mike could feel the rumblings of a small volcano inside his stomach and moved toward the toilet as fast as he could in his weakened state. "I'm gonna puke. I gotta make it."

Suddenly a corpsman appeared out of nowhere and jabbed Mike in the rear with a syringe.

"Wow, what was that? What did you do, man, shoot me?"

The corpsman, weapon in hand, grinned widely. "Johnson, my boy, you ain't gonna puke. You ain't gonna get rid of the liquid in ya; you're gonna keep it. That's it, man. You're dehydrated enough. You can't afford to lose anymore."

Sleep, massive headaches, writing home, taking medicine, cold showers, and more boredom.

The malaria ran its course, and Mike convalesced in Cam Ranh Bay. It was at a beach party with round-eyed air force girls that Mike knew he was ready to go back to the war zone. Another convalescing marine was imitating fire fight,

In front of "new" hill, south of Da Nang,
December 1967

Filling sandbags to protect base

rockets, ammo dumps blowing skyward, bullets zinging and popping. Mike could feel the surge of adrenaline.

Two days later Mike was back with his company, which was now stationed on a hill to the north of where Hotel Company had been. The old hill they had fought for was now deserted. This new hill was India Company's old hill. Mike felt the anger in his throat. It was like a game.

One evening in early December as Mike and his buddies sat in their tent playing cards, the air suddenly exploded with rapid small-arms fire. Mike grabbed his helmet, trenching tool, and rifle and scrambled out of the door and underneath the raised platform of the tent. Other marines followed.

"What can you see, Johnson, anything?"

Mike didn't answer immediately but steadily gazed down into the old, deserted village and then beyond to the new village. In the light of the flares, Mike could see movement in the rice paddies.

The marines began to pick up targets and fire back. The light from exploding mortars combined with the flares to create daylight out of darkness. Mike picked up a figure running across the rice paddy three hundred yards away. He followed the enemy with his rifle sights, then gently squeezed the trigger. The golden tracer leaped down at the man, the lead biting into the water at his heels. The man began running faster, digging desperately across the field. Mike knew he had him and gently squeezed the trigger. But nothing happened. The shell was stuck. He whacked the rifle against the tent pilings. A nearby marine shoved a ramrod in Mike's hand. He jammed it down the barrel, kicked out the old shell, and smoothly clicked in the new one. Mike picked out the man again, still running. He took aim and began to squeeze.

"Hold your fire. Hold your fire!"

Mike angrily snapped his head around to see who gave that command.

The lieutenant was running down off the hill. "Those are South Vietnamese you are blowing away. The Cong must have fired on us as their patrol was coming in." Mike felt angry disappointment. How could you tell, anyway?

A few weeks later Mike's patrol and one other patrol was taken out to a peninsula in the river by two amtracs. Some of the men scouted about and then returned with the amtracs as though they had been on a temporary mission. Mike and his men were left behind to set up an ambush. Mike found the perfect spot—bamboo hedges, lots of greenery, a clearing. They set up the ambush in an L-shape, with four marines of the machine-gun squad positioned at the top to shoot down the trail. Men were placed so they could shoot high and low in a crossfire without hitting their own men. Trip wires were set up behind the ambush so a retreating enemy would set off grenades. The trap was set up on a well-used trail that came off the river.

Night came with low clouds eclipsing the moon. Birds settled back into the trees, chirping their night talk. Mike stuck the barrel of his M-16 through the thick bamboo hedge and tried the sights. The marines swapped places quietly to keep awake. Every fourth man slept for half an hour. The marines at each end of the ambush were always awake. But no one came.

At four in the morning, Mike felt the hunter's instinctive shiver. There was movement. He sensed it before he heard or saw anything.

"But they're coming from the wrong way. They're coming from the direction of the machine gun squad." Mike knew he couldn't alert those men without giving away all positions. He could only hope they were seeing what he was seeing. Mike knotted up in a tight pulsating ball. He slowly moved the .45 in his hand into position and cocked the hammer back. He could see the shadows now, moving toward his bamboo hedge.

The small glimmer of moonlight stabbing through the clouds gave Mike enough vision to see the human shadows, rifles ready, stalking through the trees and into the clearing. Every nerve was tingling. His heart was thumping loud and hard, his breaths were fast and panting. Every muscle was alive with expectation. Mike aimed at the head of one figure who separated from the others, close enough that he could hear his footsteps in the heavy, wet grass. He began to squeeze slowly because he knew he would have only one chance.

"Johnson, Johnson, where are you?" The loud whisper came from the shadow. It was Wally Schmichle, the leader of the machine gun squad! They were coming in early.

Mike felt instantly sick. He quietly let out a long, slow breath.

"I almost got you, Wally. You were half a second from being blown away." The two sat there in silence, looking at each other, knowing and wondering how often this scenario had been played before. But after the horror seeped away, the anger was back, anger at the always-elusive enemy, the shadows they could never see, never hit.

Charlie disappeared down into the never-ending network of tunnels, and the Americans never saw any results. The marines rarely saw the enemy, yet they were always hunting, always scared, knowing their turn could be tonight, tomorrow. They saw helicopters explode before their eyes, saw fellow marines maimed and killed, fought the devastating jungle and weather and leeches and homesickness. The newspapers and Armed Forces radio constantly announced the body counts—how many Cong killed and wounded in action today; Mike wondered where the numbers came from. He tried to estimate how many pounds of bullets he'd fired on ambush or on watch—never fighting gooks eye to eye, just firing into the jungle at shadows or where a flicker passed, hoping you hit one of them, always hoping, shooting where you thought they ought to be, shooting at flashes of light from gook fire, but you never, ever saw them. Logically, he knew he had to be hitting flesh at least part of the time, but without the evidence of his eyes it seemed random, phantasmagoric. When he heard about atrocities, he knew how they happened—how the frustration could build to anger, could build to rage so that any clear target—anyone you could call the enemy—could become the focus of an act of obliteration. He understood why men drank too much, bought women, sniffed coke, set up black market deals with goods pilfered from the supply dumps. It was their way of buying relief or fighting back against the meaninglessness, imposing a little garden of purpose and control on the vast jungle of the war.

It wasn't Mike's way. He was still there to fight. He kept his body as strong and clean as he could. He kept his equipment working flawlessly. He turned aside the drinking and the drugs lightly, and after a while no one even joked about the "Mormon missionary" anymore. He had told his own patrol, "Guys, if anyone is high on pot or anything else, you don't go on patrol. You're a danger to our lives and your own. You stay home! If I ever see it again you're going on report. One chance, that's it. That's more than a VC knife or bullet will give you."

He had never had to put anyone on report for drugs. The respect from his men felt good. Most of the guys drank beer, but it was usually to try to satisfy an unquenchable thirst. In the field warm beer and sometimes Cokes were dropped by helicopter to the sweating, suffering marines. Men would grab a can, pop the top, and quickly cover the warm, gaseous fizz with expectant mouths. Mike tried it once when he was desperately thirsty and gagged on the sickening taste. He went back to the bad water from the rice paddies. Anything that looked clean he drank, and he learned to live with the resultant diarrhea. Anything had to be better than warm beer! Inside, even though Mike tried hard to live by his values, that tight expectant knot clenched harder.

Mike tried to forget the frustrations in fun days of tossing grenades into the small rivers by the villages so the skinny little Vietnamese kids could wade out and collect the fish that floated to the top. He loved the rivers. They were cold and stimulating, and there were no booby traps in the water. It exhilarated him to set his patrol in a hidden spot and then sneak over the crest of a hill to see what looked safe and where to go. Point was a fascinating place for Mike. It challenged his skills, and he loved living by his wits.

It was close to Christmas 1967. Mike had been out almost seven months. The squad was now running out of a large base and enjoying good chow and a good place to sleep. The one thing he had a hard time with, however, were all the Vietnamese on the base. He wrote to his dad just before Christmas.

"A lot of Vietnamese workers come on base in the morning and leave about dusk. It's a weird thing, Dad, to see them on the base, wondering if they are stepping off distances between the ammo dump and our tent or a certain place outside the gates to the ammo dump or mess hall. Anyway, thanks for sending my buck knife. I'm getting real good at hitting trees with the sharp end instead of the blunt end. Sure love and miss you all. Have a fantastic Christmas. Love, Mike."

Mike worked hard to make Christmas special. He had received plenty of packages containing lots of presents, chocolate-chip cookies, pound cake. He hung a Linus-and-Lucy decoration up high in the tent and strung tinsel.

But on Christmas Day Mike sat outside his tent on the high hill, viewing the American bases scattered out for miles below him and watching the hundreds of red and green pop flares

Christmas in Vietnam

bursting out. A huge lump came in his throat. That night he buried his head in his pillow. He hadn't tasted salty tears for a long time.

Mike was feeling a long way from home, a long way from the Mike Johnson he used to be. He was a good marine. He knew it. Was he still a good Christian? His values had been tested pretty severely. No drinking, though. No drugs, no women, no swearing, no smoking. The men didn't understand his abstention but they respected it. Called it Mormon magic. Yes, though he wished he were home, he felt secure with himself, knew where he was going and what he was doing. He had written to Mama and Papa, his grandparents:

"Sometimes I feel almost invincible; I know I can make it the twelve months and get out of here. I'm being careful, but I'm a good marine. I feel good about what I'm doing."

January 1968 was the month Mike held his breath for. Right after Christmas he had received an exhilarating call from Johnny Davis, a buddy back at battalion who had come out and run an ambush with Mike. It was an easy night. Nothing had happened, but poor John never slept a drop. He was so scared he couldn't keep his eyes closed. It was raining, or he was sweating, or the bugs were on him, or his leg was cramped, or his helmet was rubbing his neck, or water was running down the back of his pants. Mike had forgotten all those discomforts; he had gotten used to them so long ago. Johnny hurriedly left for battalion the next day. But their friendship flourished and grew, and on this particular night, Johnny's excitement leaped right out of the phone.

"Johnson, you just ain't gonna believe this, friend. How would you like to join me and Steve for a week of sunshine and surf and women in Hawaii?"

Mike pulled a face, then realized Johnny couldn't see him. "Sure, Davis, I know, just as soon as we get outta this man's army, you're gonna treat me on the way home. Right?"

There was a groan on the other end. "Hey, Johnson, I'm talkin' facts, man. Would you believe January fourth through the tenth? I got it all fixed up. You and me and Steve. We'll have a blast! Now, here's when you need to come into battalion . . ."

Mike drifted on clouds for a week. He let about everyone he knew know he was going to Hawaii on R-and-R. He was going to stay awake for six days and nights, spend every penny he had, and chase every round-eyed beauty he met! Barbara was coming, but he didn't plan to get serious. The two days preceding Mike's departure were filled with packing, exchanging money, asking around about Hawaii.

The jet revved its engines and swept down the runway, leaving the earth like a giant but graceful swan. Inside, three marines wore perpetual smiles; no talking, just grinning. They finally settled down.

"Oh, oh, oh, did you see that stewardess? She was beautiful, Johnson, just beautiful. Oh man, oh man, it's been too long." Johnny seemed awe-struck. He couldn't talk anymore.

Mike wanted time to move in slow, slow motion, to have everything stick with him. He wanted to grasp everything and hold on.

Mike did sleep when he got to Hawaii, about three hours a night! He tried hard to blow the $400 won in poker, and never let the rented car or 650 Honda motorcycle cool down. People gawked at the three wildly dressed young haoles roaring along the beach on the same motorcycle. And then there were girls, body surfing, sightseeing, and more girls.

"Hey, Johnny, I gotta go see Lynn tonight over at Laie. I

On balcony of a Hawaiian hotel during R-and-R, January 1968

don't want Barbara to get lonesome, though. She came all the way from the states just to see me. Think you could take Barbara out for something to eat?"

Johnny broke into an uncontainable grin. "Johnson, for you I will make the ultimate sacrifice and accept this most gruesome assignment."

The last day in paradise came way too soon.

"Well, how are we gonna wind this gig up, Mike?" Johnny was slouched in a loudly flowered deck chair on the patio, looking out at the blue and the whitecaps breaking against the shoreline, rolling in on the sparkling sand.

Mike was deep in thought. It had felt so good to be so alive; relaxed, not scared. A guy needed room to come down. Hawaii had given him that room, out on the catamaran, sitting on the beach feeling the wind, enjoying the little inland lake by the Hilton with Lynn. It had been so good. Mike grinned to himself, but there was a chill at the back of his mind. Just the night before in the hall of the hotel, some kids had set off a few fireworks. Mike had been in a deep sleep. He freaked out, grabbed for his gun—which wasn't there— and finally came around to the calming words of Johnny and the startled, scared faces of the three wide-eyed kids.

But that was yesterday, and today they would pick up the girls and body surf at Sunset Beach. The waves were monstrous, challenging. Mike bounded out into the surf, ducked under the column of crashing waves, and felt himself sucked out by the undercurrent until he was far from the girls and some Hawaiians staring out at him from the beach. The tide was absolutely awesome, with a powerful wind whipping the tops of the waves and throwing out a sheet of water.

The fifteen-foot waves caught the marines and smashed them to the bottom, scraping them along the sand. The boys went for more, laughing and yelling. After 'Nam, danger was a relative term. Exhausted, Mike stumbled through the shallow surf up onto the beach.

"Crazy—you crazy man!" Mike stared at the large Samoan with a huge Afro shaking his head. "You got white brains, that's for sure."

As Johnny bade a last farewell to his folks and teasingly pulled Mike away from Barbara, he sarcastically commented, "Let's go home, Johnson." The statement hit Mike in the pit of his stomach. Home was West Virginia—or was it? He had made an emotional break with his family home that he hadn't even realized. But Vietnam certainly wasn't home. Where was home? He was floating.

Back in 'Nam, Mike learned that his company had been moved southwest into the mountainous "Arizona" territory. This was Viet Cong country, where a company lost one or two men a day. Thousands of North Vietnamese regulars poured down the Ho Chi Minh trail. And Mike's patrol was soon seeing regular action, fighting every night and running ambushes and patrols in the day. Booby traps were all over. Because of the loss of men, squads were operating at half strength, and fire teams of two or three instead of five or six were sent out. Mike's patrol was assigned to burn villages that were known or suspected to sympathize with the Viet Cong. They would torch huts which contained ammunition and throw grenades into the holes and tunnels they found in the huts or at the edge of the jungle.

Even here, the marines never saw their enemies. They fought shadows, chased the flashes of rifle fire, shot hundreds of rounds into trees and tall elephant grass. The wounded and dead they saw were marines. The dead Viet Cong disappeared into the jungle, into the network of tunnels. Marines watched helicopters land under fire, gather in the wounded, and take off again. Many choppers were shot down, and the surviving marines desperately tried to protect them until others could swoop in to rescue the dying and wounded.

Shortly after Mike's return he almost became one of the many daily casualties.

"Hey, Johnson, move your fire team through the left side of the village." Mike quickly glanced over at the black sergeant who was motioning with an M-16.

"Okay, Sarge. We'll grab a drink and take off." Mike lowered the bucket into the well, heard the echoing splash, and hauled up the bucket filled with water. He drank deeply the cool, sweet water. As Mike finished, he sensed a metallic taste in his mouth, then dismissed the thought and barked, "Okay, group. Let's move out." Within fifteen minutes Mike began to sense a strange tightness in his throat and chest and a buzzing, tingling feeling in the rest of his body. Suddenly the tightness clamped down tightly. Mike dropped to his knees and struggled to whisper a panicked plea.

"I can't breathe. Can't breathe. Get some help." Within seconds Mike was unconscious.

"Corpsman, corpsman! Over here! Fast, man. I don't think he's breathing."

The corpsman quickly knelt beside Mike and began giving him artificial respiration.

"I'll bet it's the water in that well back there. The gooks poisoned it; Johnson drank poisoned water." Others nodded or grunted in agreement.

A chopper arrived and whisked him back to Da Nang. Mike was so sick for three days he remembered very little of the experience, but recovered quickly and was soon back with his patrol.

During this intense period of fighting, Mike earned the Bronze Star. A group of men had been pinned down by heavy automatic-weapon fire. Mike's fire team worked its way around the firing and reached them. Mike's next job was to get them out of their secure spots.

"Come on, men. Across the paddy. The company and warm grub are waiting on the other side. Follow me." Mike dashed across the paddy at full speed. No one shot him, but no one followed him either. He scrambled back just as fast, mud up to his thighs, bullets splashing water in his face.

"Okay, you turkeys!" he screamed. "I'm not doing this for my health. Follow me! Now!"

Mike crossed the paddy several times before all the marines followed. They began pushing down the trail to the rest of the company. To their right, near the tree line, a hootch (a Vietnamese hut) stood under a burned-out tree. Smoke curled up lazily from a cooking fire and showed gray-black against the skyline and the thick clouds.

The patrol leader some two-hundred yards away radioed Mike's group. "Johnson, check out the hootch over to your right. I've got a feeling about that place. Too quiet. Be careful, man."

Mike ordered one of the team to fire a couple of rounds at the base of the hootch. The clods of red dirt exploded into a haze of dust. Then silence.

Mike and his fire team assaulted the quiet hootch, firing automatic and semi-automatic M-70s up to the doorway. There, Mike leaned against the wall, checked his rifle, then swung into the hootch. An old woman and her daughter were huddled behind a mound of dirt. The others filtered in around him as Mike stared at the sickly, frightened pair.

"Johnson, there's a tunnel over here. Better have a look."

Mike quickly snapped out of his trance and moved to the hole behind the dirt mound. He pulled the pins on two grenades.

"Jones, take those women back by the door." Mike threw the grenades down the hole and covered his ears as he, too, dashed for the door. Red fire and dust rushed from the hole.

And then bullets were pouring from the jungle. Mike and the others automatically hit the dirt.

"I don't think we were supposed to burn this hootch," yelled Mike. "I've got the old woman. You bring the other one. Let's get out of this hootch. Stay on your stomachs."

The fire team wiggled out of the hootch on their bellies, pushing the two Vietnamese women out with them.

"I've got the corporal on the horn." The radioman handed the set to Mike.

"Sir, we're under fire and have two Vietnamese women here."

"Johnson, you and your men get your butts across the paddies back here. Leave the women. We'll give you cover fire."

Mike handed the set back to the radioman, then suddenly jumped as a bullet smacked into the dirt next to him. "Okay, guys, you heard the man. Let's get out of here."

Mike's long legs flew across the clearing. Massive firing boiled the water as his men followed him into the muddy rice paddies. Mike was streaking down a football field. He felt exhilarated, challenged, afraid. He pushed his lean muscles, gulped in the moist air.

He was near enough to the patrol he could hear them yelling encouragement, when he glanced back over his shoulder. He slid to a stop in the mud, turned, and charged back into the line of fire. He didn't think about what he was doing. But he had seen one of his men down on the edge of the rice paddy nearest to the hootch. Mike finally reached him across the ocean of rice. The marine lay stunned and paralyzed in the mud, totally disoriented. Mike dove into the muddy soup just as three bullets zipped into the water where he had been standing.

"You're going to be all right. Just hang on." He shoved and dragged the marine across the spongy, shallow lake. Mike, hypnotized by the adrenaline, the excitement, felt impervious to the bullets bouncing around them. He carried the marine to a corpsman and wandered off to find a drink.

The next morning found Mike and some others from his patrol in a giant helicopter heading for An Wah Air Base. Mike leaned back against the cool metal, closed his eyes, and listened to the thumping blades. He would be walking security for the patrol sweeping the road to the base. Supplies for the base came over the road, and the Viet Cong kept it mined. The marines were to keep it open. This was a big base, an important one.

That night he saw a movie, had good chow, and slept in a wooden hootch. Mike lay in the dark with his hands folded behind his head listening to a mosquito. Shouldn't be so bad, he thought. Good chow and a good bed in a wooden hootch. He was glad he had been picked.

A loud voice in the dark brought Mike back from the cozy recesses of sleep. "Let's move it, men. We've got a long way to go today."

"Hey, Johnson, what's the date?"

Point Man

"January 30, Martinez, 1968. Why?"

"I think it's my girl's birthday."

Then all Mike could hear was the plop, plop of boots hitting the hard dirt of the road. Mike watched the marines with the minesweepers, going over every inch of the road. This methodical pace was easily learned and quickly boring. The sun made the jungle steam. No clouds.

Mike was glancing at his watch—eleven o'clock—when a loud explosion ripped just to the right. He spotted the marine on the ground and stared at the bits of white, shining bone and shreds of marine green in the blasted and bloody boot. A corpsman began bandaging. A jeep rolled up from somewhere, and the wounded marine headed back to the base.

"All right, men, listen up," Mike's squad leader barked out. "I want everybody spread out another ten meters apart and get down on the line. Keep those gooks off the side of the road. Stay alert. I don't want to lose any more like that. Now let's go."

Off the marines went, up the road. Mike watched warily as he walked, but kept a private conversation going inside his brain. "I'm glad that wasn't me. I've been lucky. I'm good at seeing signs. I'd rather trust myself than have to follow someone else. I'll make it home easy. I just need to stay sharp."

Now Mike was walking up over a hill. At the top of the knoll the grass was thick, bent, and tangled. Mike hesitated and studied the area. It would be a good place for a booby trap, but Mike knew he was good. He wouldn't step on one. He had been there too long, and he knew what to look for.

Mike felt himself being hurled up into the air with the grass and the dirt and the smoke. The roar filled his body. Slowly he floated back to earth with the cloud of debris.

The smell of gunpowder and burnt grass and flesh was strong in his nostrils. His ears were ringing, but he could hear someone screaming into the radio.

"Johnson's down. Help! Someone help."

Mike felt someone gently lift his head. "I want you to say the Lord's Prayer. Can you say the Lord's Prayer, Mike?"

Mike's mind wouldn't work. He glanced down and saw that his left leg was gone at the knee. His right leg was twisted and shattered, still connected but dangling into the hole. It must be someone else's. This couldn't be his. Then something was running in his eyes, and he shut them.

5

Wheels

Mike thought it was the light that pulled him up and out of the hazy fog, a light that shone on his left hand. Then the pain came and Mike screamed. But the pain sharpened his senses and he could hear a voice, though it seemed far away.

"The anesthetic is wearing off, nurse. Let's get this job done pronto."

Screams and explosions filled the air. Mike could smell something sweet. He tried to focus on what must have been a face.

"You're in Da Nang in a military hospital. The noises are Viet Cong rockets, but we'll be okay. You're safe and we're taking care of you."

Mike's pain was subsiding into unconsciousness.

This was the first day of the Tet offensive, and Viet Cong snipers had infiltrated the hospital, blowing up wounded soldiers in their beds. After the doctors finished working on his hands, Mike was moved to a more secure area and sandwiched between two mattresses under a bed. Most of the wounded were moved into bunkers, but the doctors were afraid to move Mike. He lay still between the mattresses in the black room, deep in a morphine dream.

Mike hung on through the long night as the American military pushed the Viet Cong back. He floated in and out of his welcomed narcotic oblivion during the next two days, catching snatches of sounds, explosions, shouts, screams, and nurses in helmets.

The shivering finally woke him. He shook his head to clear the fog and tried to focus his eyes. There were rows of stretchers, at least five deep, lining the sides of a huge stripped-down jet. The stretchers were filled with wounded soldiers, some asleep, some groaning, one vomiting into a basin held by a nurse.

Mike's mind cleared for a moment. *I'm not dead,* he thought, *but I don't feel pain either. Just numb, unable to move, nauseated. And so cold. Am I going home?*

The drugs and the sound of the jet carried him off again. He awoke to the worried face of a nurse. Mike couldn't keep his eyes open, and his body began to hurt, especially his legs. A bus seemed to back right in the end of the plane. And then he was lying on one of the stretchers hanging from the side of the bus wall. Mike could hear the swish of cars passing and guessed they were on a freeway. Where were they going? Where were they taking him now? Was this America?

The corpsman standing above him was taking his blood pressure. "How you feelin', marine?"

"So cold. And my legs ache."

The corpsman stared below Mike's waist. Then he was screaming at the bus driver. "Call for an ambulance! If we don't get this guy to the emergency room, he ain't gonna make it. His blood pressure is so low it hardly registers."

In the ambulance Mike managed to lift his head to see what they were doing. He dropped back to the pillow like a stone. "They're working on my knees," he thought. "There's nothing below them. But I can feel my legs, my feet; they hurt."

The stitches in Mike's stumps had burst and he was bleeding to death under the blanket and gauze. The world began to fly. Neon lights flashed by Mike's eyes in a rainbow blur. He was rushed into the emergency room. They stripped his clothes, placed a tube down his throat, and wrapped blood pressure cuffs around his stumps. As they pumped the cuffs to control the bleeding, a thousand hot slivers of pain rushed into Mike's legs, and he screamed until he fainted.

Mike opened his eyes to three gowned women chatting at a

hexagon-shaped counter. A doctor stopped at his bed. "Awake? How are you feeling, son?"

"Scared."

The doctor was lifting the blanket and quickly unwrapped Mike's left stump. He yelled toward the nurses' station. "I need a nurse, stat! This marine needs to go back to O.R. Move it!"

The horror, the excruciating pain was repeated. No one responded to Mike's loud, pleading requests as they wrapped the blood pressure cuffs around Mike's left stump. It had broken open again. His brain, then his mouth, filled with the Marine Corps language he had refused to use.

The second time the steel stitches held, and Mike finally made it to the Philippines. He spent nine days there floating in and out of the operating room on the haze of morphine and Demerol. Then gangrene began to eat away at both stumps. Jungle rot, they called it. Surgeons had to amputate higher and higher to keep ahead. The gangrene was finally contained, but not before Mike's left leg was amputated at the hip and his right leg above the knee.

Mike's father groped around for his bathrobe. The knock at the door was incessant. He had worked the midnight shift and had just gotten to sleep. He padded through the hall to the front porch. A sick, nervous feeling swept over him as he opened the door. He met the eyes of a strained marine officer.

"Is he dead? Has my son been killed?"

"Your son, Corporal Michael Johnson of the Second Battalion, Seventh Marine Regiment, First Marine Division, has been wounded in action."

"How bad?" Then Mr. Johnson recovered his reflexive politeness. "Oh, excuse me. I'm a former marine myself. Please, won't you come in?"

The captain explained about Mike. Mr. Johnson dropped his head into his hands. He could hear himself reasoning, "No, not his legs. For a kid that loved to run and play ball and climb as much as Mike did, how could this happen?"

Mr. Johnson hesitated for a moment and looked up at the captain. "How am I going to tell his mom?" The captain volunteered to accompany him to the school where she worked.

As Mrs. Johnson stepped into the hall, she saw the military green. "Mike has been killed!" The words exploded in her brain, and her knees felt suddenly weak.

Mr. Johnson could see the terror in his wife's eyes. He hurried down the hall. "Mike has been wounded. He's not dead. He's just been wounded."

The captain drove the Johnsons home, repeated what little he knew about Mike's situation. He then explained that he wouldn't see them again unless Mike died, wished them well, and politely left.

"Not his legs. Mike can never live without his legs."

Mr. Johnson couldn't disagree.

Family came and went. The phone rang. Then bargaining with the Lord began. "There must be some mistake! Mike always has been so active. Why has this happened to him? He can't live without legs. Oh, please, let it be a mistake."

On the third day after the captain's visit, a Sunday, Mr. Johnson made his peace with God. He finally prayed, "Not our will, but thy will be done. Please make us strong enough to accept thy will." He shared that peace with his wife.

That evening the Johnsons received a telegram: "Corporal Michael Johnson progressing well, expected to recover." The telegrams came often during the next days, telling them about Mike's injuries, operations, whereabouts.

Then one Monday morning just before dawn, the telephone rang. "Hi Mom. It's me, Mike."

"Hi Dad. Oh, I'm all right. I just lost my darn legs!"

A Mormon chaplain in the Philippines had arranged the call and afterwards talked to both parents. They could hear Mike laughing in the background.

"He's watching a cartoon, Yosemite Sam, on television." Mike's father relayed the news. "What a kid. Here he has a little Red Cross nurse holding the phone for him. He tells me he is just fine. He's lost both legs, he's got a hole in his head and can't see very well out of one eye, but he says he'll be home soon, and can we do some things together. We just got a telegram telling us not to expect Mike to live. I guess they don't know our son."

Mike was lying on a stretcher and could see nothing, but he could feel the descent of the jet in the pit of his stomach. Bethesda, Maryland, wasn't West Virginia, but it was America and not too far away from family and home.

Then the nurse slipped another needle into Mike, and the familiar episode came. Mike was on a drug more powerful than

Within days of arrival at the National Naval Medical Center, Bethesda, Maryland

morphine now—Delotid. He could feel it go in, hit his heart, and spread a rush of warmth and comfort through his pain-racked body. Every three hours for weeks the welcome rush came. Who cared if it ended in drug dependence? Just three more glorious hours of relief, that's all that Mike desired. This shot was particularly wonderful. Mike was a little boy at Mama Bert and Papa Ed's home, running from room to room and bouncing on the big bed.

"Michael, don't you ever run out of energy, you little monkey?" He could feel his grandmother and smell the warm sweetness of her skin as her cheek nestled on his head.

"Corporal Johnson, I am Lieutenant Commander Stack, head nurse here at Bethesda. We are going to take good care of you and expect your cooperation. Your parents will be here tomorrow, and we need you cleaned up so you'll look respectable."

The badgering voice trailed off as Mike floated away. But an hour later the pain brought him back, and he realized finally that he was in the Bethesda Naval Hospital.

Mike's mom took her place in the chair beside him, careful not to touch his bed because the slightest movement caused such suffering. She waited for Mike between the doses of Demerol or morphine that swept away his consciousness, but also his pain.

It was harder for Mike's dad. On the first visit he looked for the handsome son who had been such an athlete. He saw a sickly face with no hair, no eyebrows, no eyelashes. He expressed his love, held out as long as he could, then muttered, "I'd better go check the car to see if I left the lights on."

Mike's parents knew that he was still fighting for his life. Mike was too consumed by the torture chamber that was his life to think about that question. He lay flat on his back, counting the holes in the perforated tiles of the ceiling. Skin was stretched over his stumps. The stumps themselves were hung with weights to fight muscle contractions. All of Mike's open wounds were stitched with stainless steel, the wire ends bristling from his flesh. The slightest movement by Mike, the slightest touch by someone else, was unbearable.

Mike learned to live from pain shot to pain shot. Pain killers would work their magic for two hours. But he had to wait three hours before the needle again slid the blessed chemicals into his body. Watching the clock, waiting, making it through became a ritual.

Mike's hands were still wrapped in gauze. But he had been told in the Philippines that everything was intact. "When I get back to the States," he told himself, "the first thing I'm going to do is learn to play the guitar."

Then they unwrapped his hands. Mike stared in disbelief. "No. Not my hands. They said my hands were okay. Not my hands." He saw hands that might have been worked over by a chainsaw, swollen, blackish blue, cut apart. The index and middle fingers and thumb of his left hand were gone. His right hand had lost the middle finger, and his ring finger was fused straight and useless. Mike sobbed into the night.

Lieutenant Commander Stack ran the ward like a battleship. Schedules, housekeeping, visitors, meals, medical care, hygiene—all demanded perfection. It grated on Mike's natural instincts. His visitors had to leave at a certain time no matter how far they had come. Halfway through a great afternoon movie, the lights would go out. Nap time! Mike hated mornings. His sheets must be changed, even though the slightest touch caused agony. She was boss. Mike thought he hated her. To see her crisp white uniform coming on the ward angered but energized him.

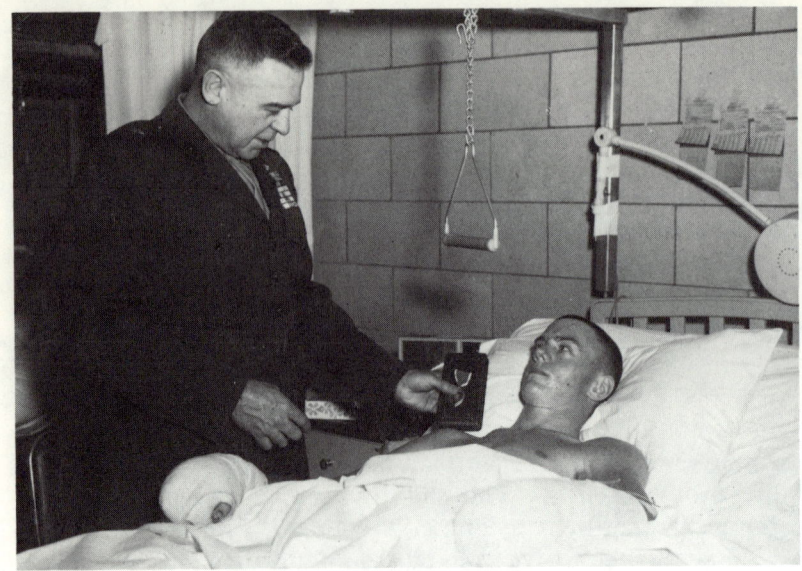

Receiving the Purple Heart from Brigadier General
Richard Johnson, February 1968

That anger, that frustration, sustained Mike for three months. And so did the love. His parents came. His grandparents came. His friends came.

He had survived. Now how would he choose to live? No one had forced him to go. He had volunteered. He had stepped on the mine. He had two alternatives, he thought, as he stared at the ceiling. He could die as he had seen others do, or he could get up and see what life in a wheelchair was like.

Mike thought of his hours in athletics. In even the tough spots when his fatigued outer self, his body, would shout, "Quit, Johnson, you don't have a chance to win," Mike's inner soul would shout even louder, "No way! It isn't over till it's over!" It was Mike's way. He couldn't quit, lie there and die; it just wasn't him. He would live because he chose to. He wouldn't die. But the pain brought him so close to it that there were times when he wanted to. It was at those *too* common times that the drugs became king! By now the soft areas of Mike's body were rock hard with scar tissue caused by weeks of shots. After a while there were no more places to stick him. Mike hated receiving the shots because of the hassle of where to put them, but he loved the instant relief they caused. He was slowly being brought down to less powerful drugs, and the weaning process left him weak, full of pain, and sick and vomiting much of the time.

Toward the end of one very bad week with very little sleep Mike lay in the dark, rolling and thrashing about and moaning. He broke into a heavy sweat, then shivered with cold. Weird, flashing dreams kept Mike's head crazy! Through the sick, flashing darkness a corpsman's voice came to Mike.

"Easy, marine, I've got a cocktail here that's real good. You're gonna sleep like a baby. There, that's gonna fix you."

And it did. The smooth, warm feeling came and Mike drifted off into a deep chemical sleep. His last conscious thoughts were of gratefulness to the corpsman who had taken pity on him.

Mike wasn't sad to leave Bethesda or the lieutenant commander. It was time to move to the naval hospital in Philadelphia for rehabilitation. He was waiting for the stretcher when he saw the crisp whiteness approaching him.

Her smile was astonishing. "Mike, I'm absolutely delighted you survived. I've been tough on you, and though it was hard, I knew I had to be for you to make it. I have a lot of love in my heart for you, marine."

She bent down and kissed the part of Mike's forehead that wasn't bandaged. He felt a warm splash against his cheek. She was crying.

"Thank you for all you've taught me, Mike, and the very best to you. You *will* make it. You're a winner."

Mike only managed a stunned smile and a weak, "Thanks for everything, ma'am. I'll remember you."

But the lady had been transformed in his memory. She had become another resource for Mike in his fight to live.

In Philadelphia Mike had to get used to being alone. The nurse had given him a wheelchair and then left. It looked ugly and old and cumbersome. He couldn't sit up in the chair because his back was so stiff and sore from the weeks of lying in bed. He could only slump or lean back. His hands were too stiff and sore to push the wobbly wheels.

"What future?" Mike spoke the words out loud, then pulled a magazine in front of his face when a one-armed, double amputee wheeled up to his door.

"Hey, you all right?" The man was leaning to see Mike through the magazine.

Mike glanced around the corner of the tattered pages and sheepishly mumbled he was okay.

Away the marine went. Mike studied the marine and his wheelchair as he sped away. He had lost more than Mike, yet he rolled down the hall with ease, pushing the wheel in long, even strokes. The wheels were connected so the left wheel drove the right one. Mike knew what he had to do.

The next day Mike was moved to one of the four amputee wards. He was with people again, marines who had all left parts of their bodies in 'Nam.

"Hey, Johnson, get out of the sack, you goldbrick."

"What are you waiting for, more legs to grow?"

"The chair's a cinch, Johnson. Just get in and let 'er rip."

Mike loved to watch the men in their cut-off pajamas zooming around. That attraction and the constant teasing finally pushed Mike into his chair. The challenge to race and "pop wheelies" soon overcame the pain.

Mike quickly moved out of the rookie stage. He cut off the bottom part of the legs of his pajamas, a symbol of his acceptance to get back into a world of activity.

"Who cares if my stump shows?" He was beginning to accept his new body.

But he still didn't have courage for the ramp, the playground of the other amputees. The ramp was the Mount McKinley of the hospital, a steep four-hundred-foot connection between the old and new sections of the hospital.

Mike went often to look but kept his distance, as the other men pushed over and down, swearing, screaming, and laughing. He knew that he would run wildly out of control and crash at the bottom. It was like looking over the edge of the Grand Canyon with a parachute on your back.

Mike had gone out one morning for a wary look down the ramp and was interrupted by an explosion of voices. Six men in wheelchairs, each holding on to the handle of the chair in front of him, rushed past Mike. They were hooting and whistling like a train. The marine in front tried to steady his wobbly front wheels with his hands. The train picked up speed as it wriggled and snaked down the ramp. "If those front wheels wobble hard enough," thought Mike, "they'll turn sideways and flip those chairs over. Those guys will be thrown out like rag dolls. They're absolutely crazy."

This happened to be a successful trip, but many weren't. The train routinely crashed. Mike would hear, "Corpsman on the ramp," and know that scraped and bloodied marines were down. He finally asked one of the train gang why they did such a crazy thing.

"I guess to celebrate that we're still alive."

A week later Mike found himself at the top of the ramp again. He knew the train schedule. They were all at lunch. Mike started cautiously, slowly, braking continuously, snaking down the slope. The pain was immense, but he finally reached the bottom.

Mike felt the tears coming to his eyes but dammed them back when two nurses came giggling toward him through the cafeteria door. Embarrassed, he wheeled in that direction. He downed some yogurt and a chocolate bar, explored the X-ray rooms, and headed back to the ramp.

"Hey, Doc, how about a ride?" Mike held his thumb out like a hitchhiker. The doctor grinned at Mike and walked right on by. Mike stared at his back in disbelief. Two nurses also ignored his thumb and laughed as they strolled by. A corpsman also sauntered by, ignoring Mike.

Then out marched a nurse whose eyes told Mike she knew her business. "Did you make it down here all by yourself?"

"I sure did."

"Well then, you're going to make it back up the ramp on your own. That's the rule. If you can make it down, then you can make it back up. You have the rest of the day to do it."

With a light reassuring pat on Mike's shoulder, she went back up the ramp. Mike stared after her.

He had no choice. Going up the ramp was like riding a cheap bike with one speed up a mountain—only worse. Mike inched back and forth across the ramp, never straight up because he was afraid of rolling backwards, out of control. His thin, weakened muscles quivered with exhaustion. His stomach muscles ached. But he finally reached his room, pulled himself onto his bed, and collapsed in a heap. He was cursing the nurses, the doctors, whoever built the ramp, and the politicians who had sent Mike Johnson to Vietnam in the first place. But he was grinning.

After the taming of the ramp, Mike attacked physical therapy and weight training with new vigor. He started harassing the new guys out of bed.

His tactics didn't work on Markham. The guy had really been blown up bad—blind, almost deaf, no legs and only one arm. His wounds were open and draining, but they never seemed to heal. A friend had bought the marine a stereo. He could hardly move and hardly hear, but he could get to the stereo controls with his one good hand—and did he love soul music! He only turned it off when lights went out. The next morning at six-thirty the Supremes would boom through the ward, shattering the blessed oblivion. The stereo had to be jacked up as high as it would go for him to hear anything at all. His deafness was a partial blessing, however. He couldn't hear everyone cursing him.

The maddening noise continued all day and into the night. The next day was the same, and the next. The men in the ward were going crazy. Someone smashed up the marine's records, another cut the electrical cord to the stereo. Anything to shut off the terrible, loud beat. But a well-meaning maintenance man fixed the stereo for him.

Finally Mike suggested, "I've been thinking. Do you think if we all chipped in and bought the kid some earphones, they would work? That way, he could hear better and we wouldn't . . ."

"Johnson, you may look dumb but you're brilliant, man, brilliant. Hey, Markham, Johnson just figured out a way to keep us from going nutso!" The earphones worked beautifully.

But the kid's body didn't. It finally just quit. Two orderlies wheeled him out of the ward to the operating room. He never came back. His stereo sat there, no lights blinking, no sound booming. No one wanted to turn it on. One morning when the ward awoke, it was gone. No one asked what had happened to it.

But life wasn't always sad and frustrating for the amputees' ward. They had their good times, too. They played the "seven dwarfs" by clowning around on their "short legs" (big wooden feet attached to short stumps for legs) and killed themselves laughing at each other. Mike hated the short legs. They hurt terribly and he felt so stupid on them that he wouldn't let anyone outside the ward see him on them.

There were high-adventure nights when a group would sneak out of the hospital or get out on forged passes.

"Hey, Johnson, some of the guys are getting out of here tonight to see a flick, a John Wayne movie about 'Nam. You coming?"

"Is the movie called *The Green Berets*?" Hardcastle nodded. "You know, I read that book once."

Hardcastle laughed wryly. Mike's mind began to carry him up, way up into the craggy cliffs of Timpanogos. It was an eternity since he had been there.

"Hey, Johnson, you're driftin' again. Think you could go?"

"I'll work on it. Gotta figure out who could lend me a pass. Sure would like to get out of this place. What time ya' goin'?"

A borrowed pass got Mike through the doors. He was out—out among the normal people, back in the real world. But he felt conspicuous, surprised, and a bit hurt by the stares of others. The company of the rest of the guys helped, and finally Mike decided he just didn't give a hoot. He was out!

The night air felt cool and refreshing on Mike's skin as he rolled up the sidewalk with his wheelchair buddies. The street smells seemed foreign but so inviting, seeming to wash away the medical stench of the hospital. The group was high, laughing and chattering about the movie, curious. What would it be like on a screen?

"Hey, guys," Jones kept saying, "this flick is supposed to be well done, real close to what 'Nam is really like, even if it is about the chicken outfit Berets! Maybe we'll even see some of the places we've been."

The amputee division literally took over the left side of the movie house, driving other spectators to the far side of the showhouse. They were loud in their anticipation and loud in their criticism. The movie was phony.

They hooted as a crashed helicopter slowly burned, giving John Wayne time to roll out of it and escape. Everyone knew how violently a burning helicopter could explode and how suddenly it could happen.

"Oh no! Look at those marines all bunched up like that, all grouped up. A firecracker would kill twenty of them. You don't bunch up like that. None of us would be here."

"Wooee, look at the booby trap, will you? Wow, look how fancy! That thing would take hours to make. It must have been made in Tijuana. Hey, Johnson, you ever see anything like that in 'Nam?" Mike laughed long and hard. It felt so good.

After a while it got funny, and they were hysterical. But in between the hilarity came times when the scenes carried Mike back to 'Nam, carrying his M-16, firing it on automatic. He just

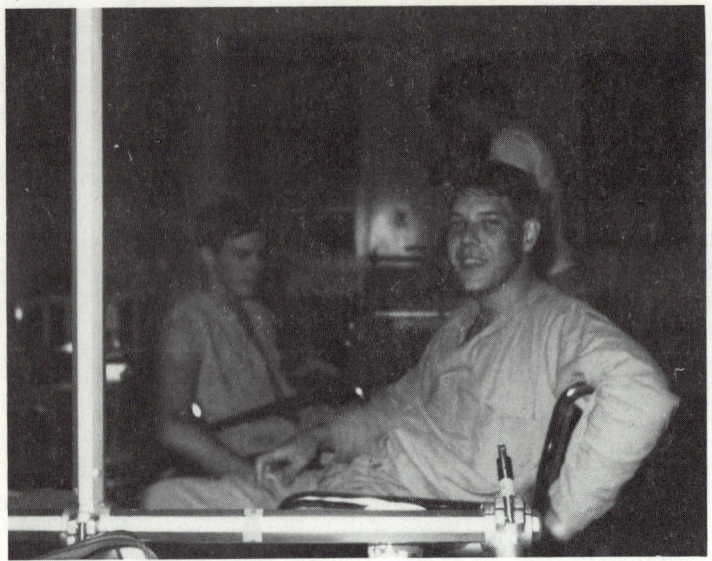
With Leo at the Philadelphia Naval Hospital, September 1968

laid his head back and let the senses ripple through him. It felt good. But he knew he didn't miss it. He knew he was ready to leave Philadelphia soon.

The best part of Philadelphia was having friends again. Vietnam had been a lonely life for the gregarious Mike. One fulfilling friendship was with Leo, a lively Hispanic who had lost a leg and eventually his other foot, but it didn't stop him. Leo had limped into the ward on canes, chatted with a couple of guys as Mike casually observed him, caught Mike's eye, and limped over to his bed.

"Hey, marine, what's up?"

"Not much. Hey, you walk pretty good with those things. Sure wish I had part of my left leg so I could try those pegs." Mike stared down at Leo's leg and foot.

Leo smiled. "Aw, you'll do fine, Johnson. No big deal. It'll come. Just give it a little time. What outfit were you with? When were you wounded?"

Mike, surprised at the instant chemistry between them, offered, "Second Battalion, Seventh Marine Regiment, First

Division, Hotel Company. In January I stepped on a mine in Da Nang Province. How about you?"

"Last year, along about October. Did the same thing." A frown clouded Leo's face. "Well, that's all history anyhow. I live in the present. You wanna go drive my car?"

The question was so unexpected that Mike was dumbfounded. He opened his mouth, closed it, and tried again. "You got a car here? Naw, you're kidding. How could you drive? You don't have a whole lot more left than me!"

An infectious grin spread over Leo's face. "Get in your wheels, man, and wait for me. I'll show you." With that Leo limped over to the door at the end of the ward and patiently waited for a fumbling Mike to collapse in his wheelchair and roll up to the door.

There it sat in the empty parking lot, a shiny dark-cherry coupe, Leo's chariot of freedom.

"Oh man, Leo, this is outasight." The excitement bubbled out of Mike.

Leo helped him frog-hop into the passenger seat with his hands, then made his way to the driver's position and explained the hand controls to Mike. He demonstrated again for the giddy Mike, then changed places. Mike caught on fast and was soon driving smoothly around the parking lot. His mouth was also in gear, his thoughts spilling out.

"Oh man, another step. If I can just get a car with these hand controls, *freedom!* I'm out of this navy prison, folks. You won't see me for a long, long time."

Mike drove and drove. He was fifteen again, driving Dad's car for the first exciting, exhilarating time. It was beautiful. He wouldn't stop until he was trembling from fatigue. "Oh thanks, Leo, thanks. You'll never know what you have done for me today." But Leo knew.

Mike hit the ward jabbering excitedly and didn't quit until he had told all. It excited the whole group, this possibility of being free again.

After that, Mike and Leo shared a lot of time together discussing life and love and families and religion. Both came from religious families, and they buoyed each other up during tough times, which occurred almost every day. Discussions ranged from Leo's Catholic and Mike's Mormon theology to why the kid three beds down had died.

"Leo, the kid wasn't hurt that bad. Sure he had lost a leg,

but so did we. He told me once he felt like such a freak, he could never go home. I don't get it. Not go home? After his operations, the guy would get down so low. He could have walked with a slight limp. He just didn't seem to have anything to fall back on during the tough times. He didn't need to die, Leo, he could have lived easy."

Leo nodded and grunted every little while to let Mike know he was still listening. Mike kept talking, groping toward meaning.

"You know, I think it was because he didn't have those blocks underneath him to lift him out of the deep water like you and me. I have so many supports underneath me I can always dig down and find something to grab hold of, like my family, my church, an inner strength, or whatever I have. I hate to quit, Leo, and the kid just didn't have any of that. I think some of those things were kind of ingrained in me from day one—the competition and everything; my whole life has been built around never quitting and hating to lose. I think you and a lot of the other guys are the same way. We're gonna fight this thing and beat it."

Utah

6
The Taste of Failure

Mike floated motionless on the rubber raft he had paddled to the middle of the swimming pool at Camelot Apartments in Provo, Utah. It was mid-morning, and the early spring of 1974 was just warm enough. He dragged deeply on the joint he was holding, keeping the sweetly acrid smoke in his lungs as long as possible.

He blew it out and relished the slight spinning feeling. It felt good. It wasn't often he felt good anymore these days. Six years since 'Nam. A lot had changed. Mormons weren't supposed to smoke pot. Well, the kind of Mormons he knew got up in testimony meeting and talked about how God had answered their prayers and let them find tickets to the football game in time. He didn't know Mormons who were trying to patch a life together with no legs. Being a Mormon hadn't helped him keep his wife or his little boy, either.

He shuddered slightly and took another drag. Denise. The hospital. The images formed on the inside of his eyelids. Casey. He opened them and stared at the sun. He had to close them again, but tears still trickled out of the corners of his eyes.

He had arrived in Salt Lake City in late September 1968, persuaded by the military adviser who had spelled out his choices: stay with the Marine Corps as a disabled vet on a pension of about $600 a month or go with the Veterans Administration—more money and more consistent medical care. He had chosen the VA route and had come to Salt Lake City, where a renowned plastic surgeon, Clifford Snyder, could work on his hands. The sight of the mountains from the air had lifted his heart, but checking in and being assigned to a ward of mostly World War II vets had pulled it down. Rock bottom had come when a nurse, staring distastefully at his chopped-off pajamas, enunciated icily: "Corporal Johnson, are you aware how embarrassing it is for those who see you exposed this way? Please cover your stumps."

Mike flinched at the memory. He had used a lap blanket for a long time after that. He dipped his hand into the pool and tried to concentrate on the feel of the water, the sensation of the sun. It was no good. X rays, exercises, dental appointments, enemas. On 5 October 1968 he was admitted to the orthopedic ward for the fitting of prosthetics. Estimated number of hospitalization days: one hundred. His chart had read like a case study invented for medical students:

> Chest. No significant chest abnormalities.
> Hands. AP and oblique views of both hands show severe bilateral injuries consisting of amputation of the left thumb, fracture of the second metacarpal, amputation of the second and third phalanges at the level of the mid-portion of the proximal phalanges, flection contractures of the fourth and fifth fingers of the left hand. On the right, amputation of the third finger at the metacarpal-phalangeal joint has occurred and severe flection contracture of the right fourth finger is present. Some metallic foreign bodies are still present in the soft tissues of the right hand. Impression: Multiple amputations, fracture and flection injuries involving both hands as described.
> Weight: 125 lbs., temperature 97.9, pulse 79, blood pressure 120/80. Head—small, depressed area in mid-forehead. Eyes—OS—multiple small foreign bodies on fundus. OD—normal eye. Nose and throat—no lesions seen. Neck—no masses palpated. Chest—clear to PVA. Heart—NSR [normal sinus rhythm]. Abdomen—no tenderness or organ anomaly. Rectal—prostate small. Skin—powder tattoo of eyebrow area bilateral.
> Extremities: Amputations: Right leg at distal femur
>   Left leg disarticulated at hip

                        R 3rd finger at M-P joint
                        L thumb at M-P
                        L 2nd finger at mid-proximal
                        phalanx
                        L 3rd finger at proximal 1-P
                        joint
         Contractions: R 4th finger 135 degrees
                        L 4th finger 135 degrees
                        R 5th finger 30 degrees
                        L 5th finger 135 degrees
Large scar anterior L forearm impression
   1. Depressed skull
   2. Traumatic amputation—multiple fingers
   3. Contractives of multiple fingers
   4. Bilateral leg amputations
   5. Foreign material—left eye
Pelvis: Re-examination of the pelvis again shows the disarticulation at the left hip, marked osteoporosis of the pelvis bones, especially in the area of the left acetabulum. Some soft tissue swelling and air in the soft tissues are noted and this would seem to indicate some soft tissue cellulitis. Because of the extreme osteoporosis, it is impossible to say whether there is actual osteomyelitis or not. There has been no appreciable change in appearance of the area since a film dated 11-4-68.
Impression: Severe osteoporosis and soft tissue swelling about the left hip indicate some cellulitis. The presence of osteomyelitis cannot be excluded, but neither can it be definitely diagnosed on the basis of this study.
Darvon every two hours. Pre-ops with Nembutal, Visterol, atropine.
Demerol for post-ops. Morphine. Vistaril.
Darvon.
Demerol.
Nembutal.
Morphine.

But it wasn't enough. Mike begged, wept, screamed for a pain shot. Infected sutures. Serum hepatitis. A mysterious malaria-like flare-up. And more drugs.

Mike turned uneasily in the bobbing raft. Dale and Patty and their two kids had been there—his cousins—when he'd

A 1969 fishing trip to Strawberry Reservoir

been able to leave the hospital in June 1969. They took him to church, treated him lovingly without pampering or spoiling him, expected him to pay his own way. A visit from his brother Steve. A trip to Yellowstone in his own car. That, more than the release from the hospital, had given him back himself.

After he had driven Leo's coupe, Mike couldn't rest until he got one. It was the top item on his agenda when he got to Salt Lake City. The VA would pay for the disability-related parts of the car—the automatic transmission, the bucket seats, the hand controls. Mike had been as restless as a caged cougar waiting for delivery that winter of 1968–69.

It was a gorgeous GTO, gleaming brown. He'd made José pick him up at the hospital so he could be the first one behind its wheel. When the engine started, Mike could feel himself trembling. Or was it the vibration of the car? It was alive, giving him back his life. "Twist for gas and push for brakes," he repeated as he got ready to put it in motion.

At the first twist, the GTO leaped forward like a thoroughbred out of the starting gate. The back tires screamed, laying down strips of smoking rubber across the street. He pushed—

The Taste of Failure

panicked—to brake, and the car screeched to a halt, throwing Mike into the wheel. When he caught his breath, he respectfully twisted the gas control. The GTO came alive again, screaming out onto the street and fishtailing all over as Mike fought to regain control. He was terrified. He was exhilarated. He was free again. He didn't leave the freeway until the gas tank was almost empty.

The trip to Yellowstone had been terrific. Mike's subversive agenda had been to see Denise. His mouth twitched. Denise. Bubbling and bright-eyed. She'd never known him with legs and seemed to accept him totally that summer of 1969. It had been easier with her than Barbara. Barbara had never stopped writing. Once he arrived in Salt Lake, she'd visited him faithfully. But once out of the hospital, Mike couldn't overcome the psychological block of the way he'd been with her before. The memories jarred against his legless present. It was too painful. He stopped calling and concentrated on Denise. Easy to talk to. Never seemed to hold anything back. Denise responded. It was a vivid, dazzling romance. When she went to West Yellowstone for the summer, her folks let out a sigh of relief. Mike's reappearance with Steve in Yellowstone started the merry-go-round again. Denise quit her job and they had a wild couple of weeks. Her folks began a round of protests neither Mike nor Denise wanted to hear, then clamped down.

Mike and Steve had driven cross-country to West Virginia, but even home couldn't wipe out the sense of restlessness. Somehow it wasn't really home. In August Mike persuaded Denise to fly out. She did it—against her parents' strong wishes that she not go. Mike's father joined the protests of Denise's parents. Did Denise realize the challenges of being married to an amputee? one still on drugs and only recently out of the hospital? Was Mike ready to make a living?

Mike groaned and twisted his head. The joint was out and he shredded it. Dad had been right. Mike's bishop had married them. His parents had rallied around and given them full support. The first months were wonderful. Mike had been delighted to find out that sex was such a high when surrounded, as he was, by a secure and loving marriage. It made him feel differently about his body. They moved in not far away from Mike's folks, and Mike became Scoutmaster. His six-wheeled Dodge Terra-Tiger gave him back the woods and adventure. It was even amphibious. When it took him up a long sloping waterfall, he knew he was on top of the world. Throwing his lap blanket into the swirling water was a gesture that meant more than one kind of freedom.

Then it was spring 1970, and Mike was accepted again at Brigham Young University. He also became Scoutmaster again. Duck hunting. Engineering classes. A trip to Canada. Dropping out in the spring of 1971. A drafting job at the Bureau of Reclamation.

January 1972. Denise seemed restless, unhappy. She seemed to be gone at odd times, and Mike wondered where all the old spontaneous chatter was. It was easy for him to leave when she was moody, though. Hunting, fishing—there was always something. Denise announced, "We're going to have a visitor come live with us in May." A home in Indian Hills, a posh residential area in northeast Provo. Casey's birth in May.

Mike swore and hit the water. The wet splashed on his face. "Casey, oh Casey." A beautiful baby. Camping, fishing, and being assistant Scoutmaster. A representative of the Utah chapter of the Disabled American Veterans came by in September 1972. Could they submit Mike's name as a candidate for the Disabled American Veteran of the Year award? "Sure. What the heck!"

Receiving the Distinguished Citizen Award at the Utah Governor's Convention for the Handicapped and meeting Dave Tadje.

"Have you ever played wheelchair basketball?"

That was all it took. They put together a team, playing in a junior high gym in Salt Lake City. Mike would go there and practice after Casey was asleep at nights. He wasn't big on TV, and he and Denise weren't talking much.

Mike groaned again. He and Denise had gone to the temple a year after their marriage and been sealed for time and eternity. He had hoped that it would make their relationship as stable and permanent as the mountains. He'd wanted desperately to do everything right. He knew he'd made mistakes as a husband, but he could never have thought of breaking the promises they had made to the Lord and to each other in the holy place. But nothing had worked. Not counseling, not trying, not endless talking. He didn't understand. He was the one without legs. What problems did she have? He got mad

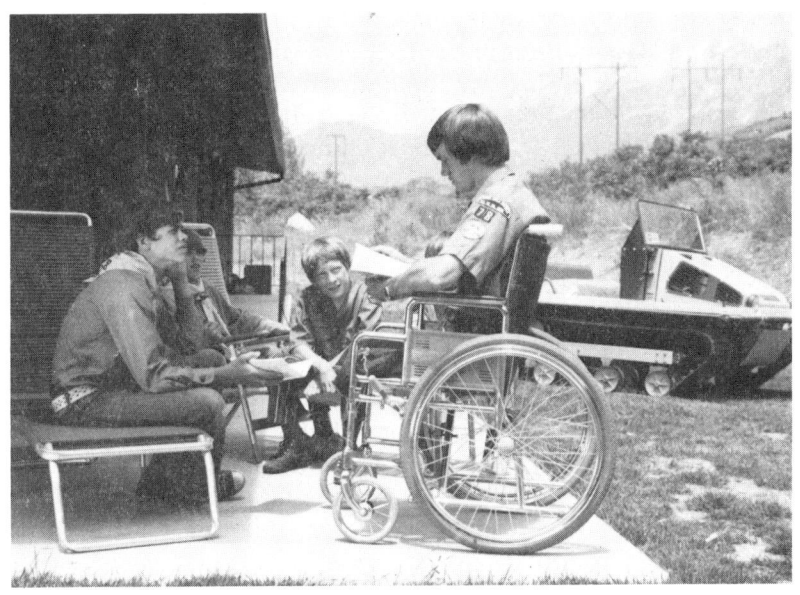

Instructing Scouts in his Indian Hills troop
(Mike's Cushman Trackster in background)

Fishing in the Provo River with friend, Del Moody, 1972

when she said things like, "It's not fun being married to you anymore." But neither one of them got into shouting matches.

Denise seemed happy, though, when he was named U.S. National Disabled Veteran of the Year. It would mean a trip to Florida in March 1973. Before it came, in February, she took Casey and left.

Mike died inside. She came back. "Let's try again." Mike's team finished the basketball season—he was the coach—with a record of thirteen wins and one loss. He was averaging thirty points a game.

They flew to Florida, dropping Casey off in West Virginia. Mike talked to Casey and Casey babbled back. Denise said nothing. The banquet was a blur. Chatting with Sammy Davis, Jr., watching the footage of the movie shot months earlier of him feeding Casey breakfast, digging in the backyard with Denise—just an all-American family—coaching the Scouts through knots in the backyard, shooting baskets, and flying over a mountain road in his Terra-Tiger. Denise disappeared during the ceremony. She didn't come back until about 5:00 A.M. She'd been thinking, she said. Walking on the beach. She wanted a different kind of marriage. A different kind of man. A week later, she took Casey and left again. Then back again. Then gone again—permanently.

Nights were hell for Mike. The sleep medications that he had been on continuously since his hospitalization increased. Seconal, Nembutal, Valium, Percodan—a handful of pills taken all at once caused dreamless sleep but also dependence. Each night as the chemical curtain dropped, Mike became a drugged zombie, the morning bringing a drugged haziness. It would be noon before Mike could think clearly. Had that bothered Denise too? She had never said anything, just seemed to accept it as a part of Mike and Vietnam.

Finally, Mike sold the house and moved into Camelot Apartments. The rest of 1973 was blank and black. So was 1974. He lived off his vet payments. He stopped writing his folks. When they called, he was terse, uncommunicative. No, he didn't want to come home. No, he didn't want them to come out. What he wanted was to die. For the first time in his life, he gave up. He'd never been interested in pot before—or cocaine or heroin or any of the other drugs floating around 'Nam. Now, in Provo, pot came, and he said, "Sure."

The Taste of Failure

All he would remember was a blue haze of marijuana smoke and rock music. No school. No work. No dates. The only thing he kept up with was the wheelchair basketball team. Every three weeks he'd get Casey for the afternoon. The night after each visit Mike would lie awake breathing in great shuddering gasps, fists clenched. Sometimes he didn't even try to go to sleep.

Mike threw an arm across his eyes. "Oh Casey, Casey." And feeling the love for Denise—still there, still wanting the togetherness, feeling it slowly die in the chilly distance between them. He had not been man enough for her, not the right kind of man. Enough of a man to marry, to father a child, but not enough to keep a wife happy, to be the kind of father to Casey that he had had when growing up.

Mike paddled toward the deck, the taste in his mouth sharp and bitter. The taste of failure.

7

Jan

A few days later in that spring of 1974, Mike met Robyn. Robyn introduced him to Susan. They were going to Israel with a BYU group in a few weeks. Why didn't Mike come? Israel? Why? Then again, why not?

That summer Mike was on a jet sitting between Susan and Robyn. Then he was in Greece. Then Israel. After a long cold winter of being shut in upon himself, not thinking, not seeing, trying not to feel, it was like a resurrection. After living from night to night, his mind suddenly stretched to encompass centuries. After being wrapped around his private miseries, Mike saw ruins that were public glories. He'd expected the entertainment and distraction of sightseeing. What Mike got was a vision. Humankind stumbling forward, individual dreams being translated into community action. He'd cried for himself and his lost loves. Now he looked at the eyes of others for the first time in months. The eyes looked back at him—sometimes in curiosity, sometimes in pity, often in fellow feeling—and he found the tears rising again. What for? For being alive? For being human? For being one of the long line of stumblers who kept moving?

In Greece Mike's friends got him to the top of the Acropolis. He bounced around on the top of that hill without his wheelchair. He didn't care who saw him or what they thought. With relief he was not thinking about himself now but about the ancient peoples who had struggled in that land. He was away

At the Acropolis

from reminders of Denise and Casey and away from the patterns of life on the floating raft at the pool. The physical distance seemed to give him the emotional license to let go, to go back with something new, perhaps back to something new.

Spiritual feelings that had been buried for months suddenly reawakened. At the group's LDS sacrament meeting held at the Garden Tomb, which is the traditional site of Christ's burial, Mike's spirit was on fire. He desperately yearned to reach out and take the fragment of bread, the sip of water, as the emblems of the Savior's crucifixion circulated. He didn't dare. He'd broken a lot of the promises he'd made to be worthy, to stay worthy. The pain was almost more than he could bear. What had he been doing to himself?

At a sunrise testimony meeting atop the Mount of Olives, the emotion-choked voices of the tour members, testifying to the love they felt for and from the Savior, counterpointed a roaring of interior voices for Mike. The months of frustration and confusion were focusing, strengthening, quickening, channeling. He felt the debris of his life washing out and away while a spring of living water, deep within, rose and flowed in a powerful, heart-wrenching passion to be clean again, in control again.

Mike thought about the months he had stayed away from church, had drifted away from people like these, from the things he really believed. As he listened to his friends that morning, he knew that he was ready to go back. All the way back!

As Mike wheeled away from the tour plane after it landed in Salt Lake City, he looked at the mountains as if he were seeing them for the first time. He moved to a new duplex in Orem, next to Provo. And then one afternoon in the fall he was looking in the mirror at Mike Johnson with a tie. Maybe it would make him look more mature. He made his way southeast through the afternoon traffic, swung the car east up Provo's Center Street, and approached the old white building at the end—the Utah State Mental Hospital.

Mike wheeled up to the front door, thinking of the last couple of months of fishing and hunting and camping. It had been good therapy, being in touch with his body, with nature, feeling the beauty and calm green heal him just as winter canceled summer and spring triumphed over winter. It had been good but it had been all for himself. Now he was tired of play, ready to reach out. He knew his psychology background and work with young men would be advantageous, but he also knew the stigma of being handicapped. The hospital administrators were cordial; but as the interview progressed, Mike could feel their reserve. After all, the youth dorm was a locked ward filled with deep emotional conflict, potential suicides, drug addicts, kids who had been severely abused by parents. They were kids who had learned early to manipulate others to survive. How was a nice guy in a wheelchair going to cope with that?

"Why, the kids would overwhelm you and take advantage of you and run away from you. If there were an emergency, Mike, how would you get to the medicine?" The short, rotund lady in her white clinical coat pointed to a white cabinet overhead on the wall.

Mike pivoted his chair, and with one quick stroke of his long muscular arms was directly under the cabinet. He sprang up the side of his chair, swung open the door of the cabinet, and stuck his hand inside. It took only a few seconds. Mike sank back into his chair holding up the bottle and looked at his interviewers in triumph. He started work the following week.

The kids were reserved at first. Who was this guy with half a body and a never-ending grin on his face? What did he know that they didn't? They should be able to get away with murder with this guy nailed into a wheelchair. There was something they saw in Mike's eyes, however, that wouldn't let them do that. It was a quiet strength, a savvy, a sympathy with hellish problems that allowed him to quickly identify with them. They let him into their lives. Mike loved the wrestling, playing with the guys on the mats. He loved the hours spent talking over problems, working out the struggles of kids who couldn't adjust on the outside and were trying to live together on the inside. It pained Mike as he saw kids who thought they were ready and had earned the right to go outside, only to come limping back, crushed and frustrated, "failure" all over their faces. Mike forgot his problems and grew spiritually and emotionally.

But when he crawled beneath the sheets at night, he still felt alone. An important part of his life was still missing. He wasn't designed to live alone.

And then she came into his life. It was a crisp November night, 1974, and thousands of fans had packed into the Marriott Activities Center on the Brigham Young University campus hoping for a great win from their Cougars. Provo, Utah, was basketball country, and the fever raged. Mike was waiting for his friends Debbie and Susan to return with popcorn. They came back with Jan Cryer.

In the next few weeks Mike couldn't get Jan out of his mind. And he didn't try very hard. He was ready to be in love. Jan was his bishop's daughter and lived just a few houses from Mike's apartment. A bright, pretty nineteen-year-old, she was a member of the Cougarettes, BYU's drill team. He also found out, to his dismay, that Jan was in a very common situation for a Mormon girl—she was waiting for a missionary who was in Japan. He was due home the next October, when his twenty-four months of service would be over.

Jan had been conducting her own fact-finding mission. She asked Susan, who had been with Mike in Israel, all kinds of questions: "What's it like when you go places? Does he open the door for you? Is it like a normal date? How does he kiss you?" Jan didn't really want to be interested, she told herself. After all, Rick would be home in a year and they planned to get married.

Jan was in charge of a young adult gathering in her own ward—not Mike's student ward—for January. Who could she get to speak? Susan suggested Mike.

The following Sunday, Jan was listening intently as Mike told his story of survival. The next Saturday found them sitting together at the basketball game. Jan had been tense before the date. Should she help Mike into the car? Would he open the door for her? What might she say that would embarrass him? As the night progressed, they shouted at the team and screamed with each basket. Things became more relaxed. Mike was used to this by now.

After the ballgame the pair drove up Provo Canyon to the mountains and pulled into Robert Redford's Sundance ski resort. A friend of Mike's was a waiter at the restaurant, and the three of them laughed and joked by the cozy fire, munching on deep-dish cherry pie. Soon Jan forgot her fears about being an inexperienced Mormon girl out with a man seven years her senior. It was smooth and easy, and she felt good.

The next day Mike and Jan went to church together. They knew people were watching them as they came in. Jan imagined people whispering, "Imagine, the bishop's daughter going out with that Vietnam vet who's been married before." "Isn't Jan still waiting for her missionary?" Mike looked up at Bishop Cryer sitting on the stand before them. When he'd come back from Israel, he hadn't held back anything. Bishop Cryer knew about Denise and Casey, about the drugs, the medication addiction, Vietnam—everything. Mike imagined the thoughts that must be going through his head. "I'm happy to help as your bishop, but to have a date with my daughter? With your background? Are you kidding me?"

That afternoon Jan wrote in her diary: "Mike is neat. He's got problems, not just because of his accident, but spiritually. I really empathize with him—a little too much, I think. I'd love to help him if I could."

Mike and Jan began dating a lot. And they began to feel the worried concern of Jan's parents. Jan called it "hassle city." To Walt and Pat Cryer, the choice for Jan seemed logical and

During a date with Jan Cryer

simple. They knew Rick; he was strongly committed to the LDS church; he would be good for Jan. They didn't know Mike well and knew more of the bad than the good.

After a few weeks Jan lay one evening on her bed writing in her diary; her mother and father softly knocked at the door.

"Well, Jan," her father began. "What we came in to talk about isn't a new subject. In fact, you're probably tired of hearing about it. But Mom and I want to explain, so you'll know exactly how we feel."

Jan's face began to tighten. "Dad, I know how you and Mom feel. You want me to throw Mike out of my life and get excited about Rick coming home. Why is everybody against Mike and for Rick?" Jan's voice got louder. "Mom, honestly, I think you like Rick more than I do!"

Jan's mom spoke quietly. "Jan, I really do like Rick. I want you to wait for him and marry him. It's true. I don't know Mike very well. Rick's strong in the church, he has a great future, and he hasn't been married before. I have always hoped you would marry someone who was being married for the first time, too."

Jan stared at the tiny ink stain on the carpet by her desk. "Mom, I understand what you're saying. It makes more sense to marry Rick. But I'm not a computer. A girl has to listen to her heart. And I have a very special feeling about Mike that I have never had with Rick."

Her father sucked in his breath. He had been waiting for his turn. "Jan, you do need to listen to your heart, but combining feelings with a little logic makes sense too. I have another concern about your marrying Mike that you may not have thought about. With Mike's former family—wife and child—there is alimony to be paid, and child support. What effect will it have on your relationship, Jan, to have x dollars taken out of every check and sent to a former wife and son?"

They talked about Mike's physical disabilities. Could and would Jan run a home and do all the chores that a husband would normally do, but Mike couldn't do? Could she have a good marriage with a man confined to a wheelchair and with one broken marriage already?

This discussion could have no conclusion. In the spring of 1975, Jan moved to a friend's house so she could avoid such discussions and date Mike freely. But things did not always go smoothly. After Mike's initial enthusiasm, he wasn't as sure about the relationship as Jan was. Denise's decision to walk out came back to haunt him. Yes, he'd been awfully wrapped up in himself and had learned a lot about reaching out to others, but had he learned enough? He didn't think he could stand the pain of failing again in an intimate relationship. What if Jan were just carried away by the glamour of his differences, confusing pity with love because of his problems? Plagued by self-doubts, he decided to do some more dating, but he didn't tell Jan. She found out anyway and was confused and angry.

A friend's death brought them closer, but then Mike left to spend some time in California and Jan moved back home. During the summer of 1975, Jan went to New York with a group to participate in the annual pageant at the Hill Cumorah. She came back with missionary zeal and a feeling that she should at least wait until Rick got back. Mike, during the same absence, decided that he wanted to get serious.

They both registered for classes in the fall, Mike still part time in his psychology major, Jan full time in her elementary education program. Mike was still working forty hours a week at the hospital. Their shared faith became one of their important joint activities. They prayed together a lot, read scriptures together, talked about what God might want for them. Mike felt the wild outbreaks of bitterness about his legs receding farther—forever, he hoped.

Rick returned in October. Jan's family blew out a collective sigh. Jan would realize how wrong she was, dump Mike, and live happily ever after with Rick. Jan dated Rick, full of anticipation. But when she was with Rick, she wanted to be with Mike. She told Rick within a week. He said he understood but didn't feel a divorcé with a child was good enough for her.

Long after Rick left, Jan sat thinking about his parting comment. She had adjusted to Mike's physical problems, but Rick had put his finger squarely on the sore spot—Mike's first marriage. She realized she felt embarrassed when people found out Mike had been married. Jan felt ashamed of herself and her fear but resolved to work at it—with time and with Mike's help.

Mike felt nervous parked in front of the Cryer home a few days before Halloween. Jan had insisted that he talk with her mother. What could he say? He had no legs. He was older. He had been married before. He couldn't get through a day without pain medication. Why should her daughter take a chance?

Reluctantly Mike hopped into his chair and wheeled to the front door. Jan opened the door before Mike, in an excess of formality, rang the bell. Her hopeful eyes gave Mike courage. He told Pat Cryer how much he loved Jan, how much her family's negative reactions to Mike had hurt her, his own regrets about the past, his pledges for the future. Pat found herself responding to Mike—the man with the ready grin and the bright blue eyes—not to the legs, the wheelchair, the spectre of a shadowy former wife and child. She found herself responding to the love between her daughter and this man.

It was harder for Jan's father. He was also her bishop. One night soon after her talk with Mike and her mother, Jan approached him.

"Dad, I need to talk to you as my bishop. Can you listen to me with your bishop's hat on?"

"How can I break up my emotions into bishop's emotions and a concerned father's emotions?" He looked into his daughter's eyes. "Okay, Jan. I'll do my best."

The discussion began safely and went well. But then Jan started talking about her frustration with her family over her future marriage to Mike. The father overcame the bishop.

"Jan, you know, a guy in Mike's position should find someone else that can . . . somebody that has been married before, someone in his own situation."

Jan ran to her bedroom, the tears flowing. She cried and cried. Her mother entered with a timid knock.

"It isn't fair, Mom, it just isn't fair," she sobbed.

Jan's mother started talking about her own conversion to the Church. Her whole family had failed to understand her then. Maybe she could understand how Jan was feeling.

"Jan, if you'll use prayer to make the right decision, I'll be behind you all the way. Your dad will know, too."

Mike decided the time had come to propose. He invited Jan to a glamorous Salt Lake restaurant. Jan accepted eagerly. When he pulled up in front of Jan's house in the Jimmy, a four-wheel drive GMC, he took the ring out of the green velvet box and slipped it over the plastic door lock on the rider's side. When Jan climbed in, he nonchalantly asked her to lock the door. The look Jan gave Mike as she spied the ring was not what he had expected.

"Oh, Michael." Jan's tone was one of consternation. "You can't give the ring to me like this. This isn't how you do it. It's not romantic enough."

Mike frowned but recovered. "Okay, give it back and I'll give it to you somewhere else. We'll wait till we get to the right place."

Jan's lips curved up in a smile of satisfaction. She was going to have Mike do this right, over a beautiful candlelight dinner. That was the way Jan had always envisioned becoming engaged, with the diamond sparkling in the soft, flickering flame of the candle. That was the description she wanted to give to her fellow Cougarette drill team members when they passed the candle for her.

But Mike wasn't about to wait until he got to the restaurant in Salt Lake City. He quickly pulled into Ferg's Gas and Goodies on the pretense of buying gas. He turned around to face Jan.

"Jan, will you marry me?"

Jan looked at Mike in astonishment. "Mike, you can't ask me here. This isn't the right place."

They continued on toward Salt Lake City. After a few more miles, Mike couldn't stand it any longer. He pulled into a rest stop, drove over the curb and over the grass to the back of the rest area where they were alone. The determined set of Mike's jaw told Jan she was in trouble. The proposal just wouldn't wait for the romantic restaurant and the flickering candle.

"Okay, Jan, I've had it. This is it. I'm not driving any further unless you tell me if you'll marry me. I've got to know."

Jan's face softened. "Of course I will. But you could have asked me at the restaurant."

Mike broke into a wide, relieved grin. "Nope, I want the ring on you now."

The dinner was romantic enough for Jan, and Mike was relaxed enough to enjoy it.

Mike and Jan both wanted to be married in the temple. They believed a temple marriage could promise them an eternal marriage, not just an earthly one. But only active Mormons in good standing may go into the temples. Mike's first marriage was a problem, as was his life-style before he started dating Jan. Mike worked with Bishop Cryer to get the clearance he would need to go to the temple.

In late November 1975, Jan returned from a date to find her parents waiting for her.

"Jan, I got a letter from Church headquarters today." This was her father's bishop voice. She thought of conversations with her father in the past couple of weeks. What would she do if Mike's temple clearance didn't come through? Of course she would wait, she had told him. She and Mike would be married only in the temple.

Her father looked at her somberly. "Well, Mike's going to have to wait another year before he can be married to you in the temple."

Jan swallowed hard and tried to be brave. "Well, I guess I'll just have to wait then." Inside she felt sick.

Walt Cryer could contain himself no longer. He gave his daughter a big wink. "The clearance came through today, Jan. You and Mike can set the date anytime you want!" Jan whirled about, let out an uncontrolled yelp, and threw her arms about her father's neck.

They set the date for December 19, three weeks away. Plans began. What about a traditional reception line? Jan joked, "Here's what it will look like, Mike. Head, head, head, head, drop, head, head, head, head." After a good laugh, Mike and Jan agreed to an informal open house. Their friends could come and visit and put gifts under the Christmas tree.

Mike and Jan, December 1975

The wedding day dawned crisp and clear and beautiful. The blue winter sky dropped down to silhouette the magnificent mountain backdrop and the beautiful outline of the temple in Provo. The day was perfect—it needed to be. Jan's family was there, and Mike's mom and his ninety-year-old grandmother had come from West Virginia to be with Mike and Jan. Mike's father had wanted so much to come, but work commitments hadn't allowed him to. The mothers really hit it off well together, which gave Mike and Jan a lot of comfort.

In the temple the couple knelt together and looked into mirrored reflections that extended into infinity—for them, symbols of an eternal marriage.

That afternoon, after a tremendous outpouring of love and affection by their families, Mike and Jan roared off in Mike's painted up, balloon-decorated Jimmy, heading north up Provo Canyon to Midway, the "Switzerland" of the American West. They rode in silence for a while, each enjoying the winter canyon scene and lost in their own thoughts. Mike's thoughts were emotional and deep. It was so good to be Mormon, to be active and strong. He had been so wrong, back there on the rubber raft at Camelot Apartments. The Church was a beacon of light in showing the way to a solid marriage, a successful life. This time he would allow the light to guide him!

Mike looked over at Jan, desperately wanting to tell her the ideas going through his mind, but not knowing how to put his emotions into words. He didn't have to. In his eyes shone the message, and Jan's eyes radiated her own message. A hand squeeze added everything else that needed saying.

8

Back on the Track

Mike went back to work at the state hospital, and Jan went back to the university. They spent evenings going to dinner or a movie, window-shopping, or participating in wheelchair basketball. In January 1976 Mike added full-time school to work and basketball. He began taking more psychology classes. It wasn't easy.

Mike could remember charging up the stairs of buildings which had now become inaccessible. It took weeks before he learned where to find the ramps, which bathrooms he could manage. Mike would work out his class schedule, then drive around to find the buildings and the classrooms. He would count the stairs involved, check whether the wheelchair would fit through doors or into rooms filled with desks. In some buildings Mike would have to ask people to carry him up flights of stairs. He never could get used to the stares of students who didn't understand.

Mike divided people into groups based on how they reacted to his handicap. First, there were the robots. Some would stare at something far in the distance as they neared him, their eyes not wavering in the least. But Mike knew that as soon as the robots got fifteen feet beyond him they would turn their head to make sure their peripheral vision had really seen what they thought it had. Mike took care of the robots by turning around to wait for "the look," a big grin on his face. The robot usually turned red and scampered the other way.

Then there were the gushers who would run up to Mike

with, "Oh, you wheelchair people are so wonderful," or, "Oh, how do you cope with all the problems you must have? You're simply marvelous." Mike couldn't handle much of that and went quickly on his way.

Then there was the king of the hill. He or she would stand next to Mike, looking straight down at him as they talked. Mike either had to talk to their navels or get a terrible neckache.

There were the space cadets who totally ignored Mike when he was in a group. If Jan was with him, they would talk to Mike through her, as if his lack of legs mandated the need for an interpreter.

The groupies would go silent as Mike passed. Then the loud comments would begin. "That guy must have done this and that." "I wonder how he gets around in the snow." Mike always thought, "If they would just come and ask me, I'd tell them how I get around in the snow."

Mike's favorite people were the ones who talked to him normally, who weren't afraid to hunker down at his level and ask him how it was to live in a wheelchair. He understood how some people who lived in wheelchairs were always upset with others. These were the people who had a chip on their shoulder and were always ready to fight, yet they couldn't win, ever. They were always ready to badmouth someone. They couldn't see that everyone is different, with different moods and different reasons for being down. They seemed to take everything so personally, and in the process made it rough on the other wheelchair people.

But amid all the adjustments of school and teachers and fellow students, there were bright spots. Many were very understanding and treated Mike like any other "normal" student. That's the way he wanted it. One day Mike was reading the campus paper and chuckled over the following letter to the editor:

DESIGNER DEFIED

Editor:

I defy the man who redesigned the bathroom doors for handicapped (main floor HFAC) to sit in a wheelchair, open the doors, and still have a reason to go in.

Sincerely,
A Concerned Student

Mike had his private struggles, too. Sleep never came without drugs, and even then not easily. Many nights as he lay listening to Jan's quiet breathing, he would drift back to Vietnam and beyond to the life he might have lived if he hadn't joined the marines. Some nights Mike would feel anger, but anger for what? He saw vets on television who seemed to feel rage toward Uncle Sam and the Vietnamese and America and everyone else. He read about the vet who sat on his back porch day in and day out, lighting matches and throwing them in a pail. Then there was the vet who went berserk in a shopping mall and killed several people. He didn't feel that kind of anger.

Maybe he was angry at these angry vets. He wanted to get on a television station and say, "Hey, the majority of vets are just normal, everyday guys who have jobs, love their families, and are trying to make sense out of life just like everyone else." That's what he'd say. "We aren't crazies who can't be trusted. We still love America. I'm proud to be an American. I'm proud I served in Vietnam, even if the war was a terrible mistake. The doughboys from World War I, the World War II vets, even the Korean vets were given heroes' welcomes and lots of help after the war. How come we're different? Why are we part of a bad nightmare America wants to ignore and forget?"

He read all the newspaper interviews with vets, the magazine articles, the books as they started coming out. He was obsessed with Vietnam, fascinated with the whole topic—not the politics and not the military strategy but the experiences that other men had had there. He read for the flashes of recognition, the "yes, that's how it was" feeling of someone else who understood. Some of the things he couldn't relate to. He was puzzled by the veterans who couldn't wait to get out of Vietnam but who reenlisted, feeling that somehow they no longer belonged in the United States. He wondered if that would have happened to him had he come back whole, but somehow he didn't think so. He always had a home, always would. He wondered if he might have been hooked on the combat adrenaline if he'd stayed longer, turned into one of those killing machines that only comes alive under fire. Again, he didn't think so. He went back over his memories, the never-ending fatigue and frustration and the falling apart as the jungle whittled at him. Yes, people had certainly died as a result of what he'd fired into the green walls, but he didn't have the memory of anyone falling before his shot. Would it make a difference if he had?

Back on the Track 117

Again, he didn't think so. It was part of his life. He'd been confident and competent. But he sensed no desire in himself to become a professional soldier. He'd done what he needed to do —what he was trained to do. But it was a part of his life that was over. Over.

There were too many how-comes in Mike's mind to sleep gently, peacefully. But he learned to get through these long nights. People would say, "Let it go. It's over, Mike." But when a man leaves half his body in a foreign country, it's tough to let go.

Some changes were more welcome. The Cryers, not just Jan, had married Mike. They let themselves love their new son, accepting and welcoming him. One day, Jan's mom was cleaning up the garage and discovered Mike's sleeping bag, which one of her children had borrowed, and a pair of socks. She rolled them up with the bag and walked down the street to Mike and Jan's apartment. She had almost reached their door before she stopped with a start. "Hey, Mike doesn't wear socks!" Soon she was in their apartment, laughing with them.

One afternoon Mike and Walt Cryer went shopping for a camera lens. The shopping trip took them to three stores. At each stop Walt would climb out of the car and pull out the wheelchair. Then Mike would jump in and wheel into the store. Then they would repeat the routine in reverse order, ending with Mike folding up the chair and shoving it into the back seat.

At the fourth store, Walt leaned toward Mike and said in a matter-of-fact tone, "You know, Johnson, you're a real pain." They roared with laughter all the way in. Mike felt nourished, fulfilled by this new relationship with his father-in-law and he appreciated it deeply.

One cold windy morning in late January 1976, Mike was crossing the campus. The sharp echo of a wheelchair dropping onto the frozen snow snapped Mike's head in the direction of the parking lot. He saw a lithe, legless man vault effortlessly from an old Chevy into a wheelchair. The young man, sitting tall in his chair, grabbed some books off the car seat, slammed the door, and with sweeping movements of his arms, powered his chair up over the curb and down the sidewalk. Mike saw "athlete" and "basketball player" with every powerful stroke the stranger gave his speeding wheelchair. Mike was constantly on the lookout for recruits for wheelchair basketball.

All he needed to do was discover who the stranger was and convince him to play.

When the young man returned to his car that afternoon, he found a piece of paper under the wiper blade on the windshield. At first he thought campus security hadn't noticed his handicapped sticker. But it wasn't a ticket. It was an invitation to try out for the "Utah Rimriders" wheelchair basketball team and was signed by Michael Johnson. He had heard of Johnson and his wheelchair basketball team; but he wasn't sure how he felt about the whole thing, and he ignored the invitation.

Meanwhile, Mike asked a few questions. He found out the young man's name was Curtis Brinkman. He had lost his legs in an electrical accident when he was fifteen. A couple of weeks later, Mike recognized Curt's car in the parking lot. A girl sat behind the steering wheel. Mike wheeled over to the car.

"Hi, my name's Mike Johnson. I've been trying to meet Curt Brinkman. This is his car, isn't it?"

She flashed Mike a captivating smile.

"Hi. Yeah, this is Curt's car. I'm Bonnie, Curt's wife. Can I help you?"

Bonnie had walked into it! Mike began working on Bonnie to get Curt to play with the team. Bonnie felt good about Mike and had wanted Curt to become more involved athletically. It seemed like a natural. Bonnie finally persuaded Curt to join the team, and a competitive friendship soon developed.

Athletics had always been the mainstay of Mike's self-confidence. He grew surer of himself with each game. Opposing teams quickly learned that Mike was the shooter and would beat them if left alone. Mike was double- and triple-teamed, was smashed into, and was dumped out of his chair. Opponents broke spokes in his wheels and gouged his hands and arms. But he loved every minute of it. The fiercer the competition, the better.

Curt Brinkman was a great teammate. He and Mike competed on the basketball floor even though they were on the same team. The competition went on into the night in their motel room. Mike and Curt always shared the same room, and all the team would crowd in. Then the great leaping contest would begin. Mike and Curt would place the beds a distance apart. One of the pair would begin bounding up and down, then spring across the gap between the two beds. Then the

Practicing his jump shot (from a trampoline)

other would try. The distance between the beds was slowly increased. Soon the whole place was in an uproar, with Curt and Mike bouncing, leaping, and laughing uncontrollably. One of them would finally crash onto the floor.

The last important game of the 1976 season was played against the Crushers from Craig Rehabilitation Hospital in Craig, Colorado. The Utahns had never beat the Crushers, and to do so would give them a winning season. But it would be tough. The Colorado crew were big, tough, fast, and experienced.

The game began as Mike expected, fast and rough, with the Crushers pulling off the little tricks they were so good at. They would lock the Utah players up by sticking their footrests into the Rimriders wheels, busting spokes and sometimes dumping the man out onto the floor. Other times the players locked up would have to bounce around, trying to shake loose. It was a foul but hard for the referee to see and call. First the Crushers broke into a lead, then the Rimriders would claw their way back. The lead changed hands several times. As the game wore on, the screens became rougher, with metal clashing and grating against metal. Both teams were playing a full court press, man-to-man. Lots of yelling and chatter filled the air. Dale Sadler would come roaring at Mike, always talking, always intimidating. Mike would talk back, let Dale know he wasn't going to run. Mike would break out of the crowd and wheel to the side, get set to take his shot only to spin instantly to the right ten inches. It was just enough movement to throw off his shot. One of the opposing team had tipped Mike's chair with his footrest, a foul but tough to catch. It happened time and time again. Now the Crushers were pulling ahead. Finally the whistle blew to end the twenty-minute half. Mike wondered about the time, but the official timekeeper kept time by his wristwatch. Mike squinted over to the blackboard to check out the score—32 to 22 for the Crushers. At least they were within striking range.

On the first play of the second half, the Crushers controlled the tip, and the chairs all rushed toward the Rimriders' basket. An opposing player rushed into the key beside Mike. Mike decided to play a little deception himself, reached down low and held on to the opposing player's wheel. The man knew he was crowding the five-second time limit and struggled to move out but couldn't. The whistle blew. Mike's face broke into a mischievous smile. Play went on, fast, powerful, emotional. The crowd was large for a wheelchair basketball game and very vocal. The noise hyped the players and spurred them on. As the score see-sawed back and forth, the competition intensified. Curt Brinkman then received an outlet pass from the rebounding Dave Tadje, streaked by Jerry Deats, and went in for a lay-up. The Utah crew went ahead. Colorado stormed back up the court. Sadler set a screen on the right side of the court. Dave Whitely saw who the screen was for and moved in quickly. Big Halvorson of Colorado moved toward the screen, powered Whitely directly into Sadler, spun around the two collided chairs, quickly moved to the center of the key, and shot a swisher. The score was tied again. Mike quickly called a time-

Mike scores for the Utah Rimriders

out and explained to the guys that the only way they could stop Halvorson was to snub the front of one chair to the back of another to keep him out of the center. "It's the only way, guys, or he'll beat us out." It worked, and Halvorson was forced to take his shots from outside.

Now little arguments from hot emotions began to sizzle. Then a full-blown fight erupted when one of the players had his hand crushed between his chair and the chair of an opposing player. Finally play resumed. The second half was almost gone, just seconds left, when Mike was fouled and went to the foul line. The score was tied at fifty-eight apiece. "Two more points will ice the game," thought Mike, bounced the ball twice, brought it back and flicked his wrist for a high, arching shot. Swish. It was such a pretty sound to Mike. The pro-Utah crowd screamed. Mike scored the next foul shot, feeling great relief that they had pulled off a victory. Suddenly a Colorado player threw a long pass to Mike Elix who was streaking down the floor. He grabbed the ball and shot it, almost in the same motion. The whistle to end the game cut through the air. All eyes were on the ball, seemingly suspended, then swish. Elix had tied the ball game for the Crushers. One overtime was played and it ended in another tie. The second overtime was brutal—smashing chairs, straining bodies, fiery tempers. With only seconds to go and a tied score, Utah rammed a bucket home and finally won the game 68 to 66.

At the game's finale, tempers cooled quickly and joking and visiting began with players and family. Jerry Deats of Colorado sought out Curt Brinkman by the bleachers.

"Hey, Brinkman, if you could control that crazy chair of yours, you might be a decent ballplayer."

Curt grinned at Jerry, "My day is coming, Deats. When it does, look out!"

Jerry smiled, then replaced the smile with a more serious look. "Hey, Curt, all kidding aside. Have you and Johnson ever thought of competing in wheelchair track and field? You're both awfully fast and I think you'd do okay. In fact, you could really do something with your speed if you learned to control your chair."

Curt was puzzled. "Jerry, I've never even heard of wheelchair track and field. You mean they have events and meets just like regular track and field?"

Curt was so excited that the next day he sent for entry forms from the regional office. Mike caught fire too. The next track meet was the Rocky Mountain Regional Wheelchair Games in Denver, Colorado. When Curt mentioned that the track meet was April 30, only a few weeks away, Mike's eyes grew large. They had very little time to prepare, and spent many days at the BYU stadium wind-sprinting up the ramps and around the track, racing each other, working on specific events. Members of the university track team would watch, offer advice, even climb into the wheelchair to heave the javelin or discus.

In the last days before the meet, Mike pushed his chair all the way home, over five miles of uphill, lopsided, traffic-filled roads. Jan was sure Mike was going to get killed. But he didn't, and his time got faster and faster. Finally it was the end of April.

Mike and Curt were disappointed to find out that they would be competing in different classes. They had assumed, both being amputees, that they would be competing against each other. But the officials, after examining them both, had

Back on the Track 123

put Mike in class four and Curt in class five. Mike's left leg was off to the hip and he was missing some fingers. Body balance was also checked. Mike was supposedly at a big disadvantage.

The first event in Mike's class was the javelin. He had never thrown one. Knowing he had nothing to lose, Mike borrowed a javelin and began throwing it on the sideline, out into the football field that was the practice area. His throws were poor, and Mike knew it.

"Hey, man, what are you holding your stick like that for? Don't you know how to hold that thing?"

Mike whirled around to stare at a man wearing a top hat and sitting in a wheelchair.

"My name's Harvey. I'm from Hawaii. I don't mean to be butting into your business, but I'm the current record holder in this event and know a little about it. Your style is lousy!"

"So, tell me what to do."

Harvey taught Mike how to hold the javelin with a circled finger, how to cock his arm and flip his wrist, throwing the javelin like a baseball.

Harvey went just before Mike. Mike watched carefully, analytically, as Harvey wheeled his chair onto the revolving metal disk situated in front of the official throwing field. A nylon strap equipped with two metal claws was placed over each wheel, then tightened down to secure the wheelchair to the disk. Two assistants spun Harvey into position. Mike studied Harvey as he sat in the secured wheelchair facing the throwing field. All the javelin throwers threw from this position. As Harvey reared back as far in his chair as possible, then suddenly thrust his body forward, his arm and hand whipping the javelin through the air, Mike's competitive mind was searching for the way to beat him. The throw was over fifty feet.

Harvey sat on the sidelines looking smug. Mike improved with each of his three throws—thirty-two, forty-two, and finally forty-five. That placed him in the top three.

Each of the three would now have another three chances. Harvey made his first throw. Again the javelin sliced into the lawn well past the fifty-foot mark. The next contestant was far short of Harvey. Mike's swooshed past the fifty-foot mark, but shy of Harvey's toss. The next round brought the same results. The third round looked like another repeat.

"Johnson, Mike Johnson up."

A track assistant strapped Mike's chair down on the metal disk, spun him around, then asked him which way he wanted to go to throw the javelin.

"All right, rotate me around just opposite to everyone else, so the back of my chair faces the throwing field. I'll throw the javelin from the back of my chair!"

The assistant eyed Mike suspiciously. "You can't sit that way. I think it's against the rules."

Mike's jaw jutted out. "Why not? Where in the rules does it say I can't sit a certain way? I'm facing out the open end of my chair. The only difference is I'm facing opposite to the throwing field. I want to throw the javelin out this end!" Mike jabbed at the back of the chair with his thumb.

The assistants were perplexed and called in the national chairman of the National Wheelchair Athletics Association, Cy Bloom. He was a tall, ruggedly built man who used authority in his voice.

"He can throw it any way he wants as long as his leg doesn't touch the wheel, he's not turned around in his chair, and he doesn't come out of his chair. Go ahead, Mr. Johnson."

Mike reached his left arm up over the back of his chair and grabbed onto the left back push handle. With a sudden powerful pull of his left arm and a thrusting twist of his body, he whipped his right arm in slingshot fashion over his left shoulder and toward the throwing field. He released the javelin at the peak of his thrust, the force of the movement hurling his body over the back of his chair, where he hung suspended. Mike flexed his neck upward, his eyes following the javelin as it soared over the heads of two astonished judges and easily passed Harvey's mark.

The crowd cheered wildly, and Jan went crazy. Harvey looked very upset. Mike was ecstatic. This was the first athletic contest he had won since Vietnam.

The next event was the slalom. Mike had never even heard of the wheelchair slalom, let alone seen or competed in one. His eyes ran incredulously over the course, the steep ramp, the two elevated four-by-fours, the bright red cones. He stared at the customized wheelchairs his competitors were wheeling in, smooth, cut down, tilted and cambered wheels. Mike thought of his own heavy, old-fashioned chair and groaned.

Mike took three practice turns through the course, through the bars, up the ramp. He felt more ready. Mike watched the

A creative approach to the javelin throw

first competitors grunt up the inclined ramp and carefully line up their tires before moving onto the two four-by-fours. Two of the entrants ran their wheels off the four-by-fours and crashed to the ground below. Then there were barriers to jump, sand to plow through, bars to go under, cones to weave around, more ramps and configurations, little cubbyholes to back into and shoot out of. Mike watched others falling off, creeping along, running over cones, grunting up to the top of the ramp, spinning a 360-degree turn and heading down the other ramp.

Mike sat in his chair nervously rubbing his hands together, chewing on his moustache. He was surprised at how slow many of the times were. Harvey, the fastest, wasn't volunteering any pointers this time around.

The announcer boomed out Mike's name. He wiped off his wheels to make them stickier and readied himself at the starting gate. He glanced over at Jan, whose face was drawn in anxious expectation, and then nodded his readiness. The pistol exploded, and Mike was off. Up the ramp he sped with long, powerful strokes. Across the four-by-fours he glided as though his wheels were on a track, then through the bars and up on the ramp. He spun around and shot down to curve around a ninety-degree turn, zig-zagging through the cones. None fell. The officials watched with increased interest.

The crowd was cheering now. Out of the corner of his eye, Mike could see Jan running back and forth along the sidelines, screaming encouragement. After the cones Mike whooshed through an obstacle tunnel, tucking in his arms so he would knock nothing over. Then he hit the thirty-yard sprint and gave it everything he had. He flew down the stretch and across the finish line. The crowd went wild, the timers were astounded, and Jan could hardly contain her excitement. Mike was forty-five seconds faster than anyone else in any class. A new slalom star had been born. Two events and two gold medals. Mike and Jan couldn't believe what was happening.

The next event was the 100-yard dash outside on the track. Mike had heard about the speedsters and their quick chairs. But the slalom had taught him that he could compete with the best. Then he thought of his competition. They had all been running track for four to ten years, and this was his first meet.

"Runners to your marks." The announcement snapped Mike out of his thoughts. He quickly moved to the starting line, eyeing the starter carefully. Mike had always tried to get an edge by watching the pitcher, the hitter, or the runner. Mike's

Back on the Track

With Curt Brinkman (right) during a rest period at the Rocky Mountain Regional Wheelchair Games, 1976

body had changed, but his competitive know-how had not. Something told him that the starter was the key. *I've got to watch his rhythm, his timing,* he thought.

Mike shot out of the starting gate at the pull of the starter's trigger and was almost immediately twenty yards ahead of the pack. He tore down the track at a speed that even surprised himself. He zoomed across the finish line with no one even close behind. His third gold medal!

During the rest period, the other competitors pulled from Mike all the information about him they could. Where was he from? How long had he been competing in track and field? Then Mike was called to the 880-yard race. He had never run an 880 and so knew nothing about timing and distance. Did he have the staying power? Would he have enough strength left to sprint at the end? Would his heavier chair hold him back in a longer race?

The starting pistol barked out its message, and the racers were off down the track. They started fast, jostling for position on the inside of the track. Mike's start was excellent. He didn't know how to run the race, so he decided to stay behind the leader for a while, see how he was feeling, then go for broke on the last stretch. But Mike didn't like holding himself in check. He decided to let go and run his own race. Mike's muscular arms pumped downward with powerful strokes that sent his chair speeding past the leader. He let his body dictate the speed. The freedom was exhilarating, nourishing. Mike breezed over the finish line with wind to spare, feeling spent but not exhausted. As he and Jan rejoiced about another gold medal, the announcer boomed out the announcement of Mike's victory, hesitated, and then continued.

"Ladies and gentlemen, the time Mr. Johnson just ran in the 880 was only eleven seconds off the national record."

Mike stared at Jan in amazement. "Mike, can you believe it?" she gasped. "This was your very first 880—and in your heavy old chair."

"If I learned how to run this race, Jan, and really trained for it, I could go all the way!"

Mike's final competition was in ping-pong. He had learned the game from his dad, who had won a tournament in China during his tour as a marine after World War II. Mike worked his way through the tournament, slamming and spinning, until he was in the finals. His opponent beat him out in the last game of the three-game series. To Mike's four gold medals was added a silver, but he didn't even feel disappointed. His thoughts were already on next week and next month and a training schedule and a new chair.

Mike and Jan were ready for a celebration. The Brinkmans were more subdued. Curt hadn't done as well as Mike. Though he was happy for Mike, Curt's heart just wasn't in the celebration. But the next day, all were ready for the awards banquet. After the meal, the awards were presented by a Denver Broncos superstar. Mike was doing more talking than listening when the presentation was made to the outstanding male athlete at the meet. As soon as Jan quit screaming, she told Mike what was happening. Grinning and dazed, Mike wheeled to the awards table amidst a thunderous ovation. The rookie from Provo, the budding athlete who had been sidetracked when his legs were blown off, was back on the track.

Reporters nabbed Mike. Two television stations taped interviews. Cy Bloom, an official for Wheelchair Athletics, talked to Mike about playing wheelchair basketball for the United States team. Everyone expected to see him again. And Mike expected to be there.

9

Garnering the Gold

One hot night in early June 1976, Mike and Jan tossed in bed in their hot apartment. Suddenly Jan seized Mike's hand and pressed it to her abdomen. "There!" she breathed. "Can you feel it?"

Mike could. He'd been pleased when Jan had told him in April that she was pregnant, but his reaching out in pleasure met the pain of his memories of Casey, and he'd been more happy for her than with her. When he felt that flutter under their laced hands, the jolt went straight through his body. He opened his mouth to say something and found himself sobbing, clinging to Jan, whispering brokenly over and over, "I love you, Jan. Oh, I love you."

Long after Jan had fallen asleep, Mike lay staring at the dark corners of the bedroom. Now another life was coming into his, and he was too excited to sleep. His thoughts drifted toward home in West Virginia and life before 'Nam. He felt little twinges of homesickness and thought it strange to have those feelings. Home was very important to Mike. Slowly the inspiration grew. Even though he now had a great marriage, was deeply in love with Jan, and they had a baby joining them, the feeling wasn't complete. Something was still missing. Home—a home; what they needed was a home of their own, a house that was theirs. Maybe that's what the feeling was, a need for roots. They would go house hunting tomorrow! With that decision, Mike fell asleep.

That summer they found a home in the small town of

Training at Cougar Stadium, 1976

Alpine, nestled against the base of Mount Timpanogos at the north end of Utah Valley.

Mike poured the energy of happiness into his training. Their next meet was the San José regionals, which would select the best in the West, who would then go on to New York in mid-July to the national finals. Mike and Curt trained their hearts out, determined to make it to New York. They wheeled the back roads, lifted weights, and did windsprints up thirty-foot ramps. They also looked for a sponsor. Wheelchair athletes have to be self-supporting, but nothing clicked until just a few days before they were supposed to leave. Someone told them that the kids at Scera Park Elementary School in Orem had heard about their plight and had taken on the project. With only two weeks to go, the kids had mowed lawns, shined shoes, held car washes, and raised $1,193.43. Other schools had pitched in with an additional $4,290.00. At a school assembly Mike and Curt staged a hot-wheels exhibition that got a standing ovation, then signed autographs.

It was much more than the solution to a financial problem. Curt said that it was one of the most touching things he'd ever seen. For Mike it was an outreach from kids who didn't even know him, and something—perhaps the love already filling his heart for Casey and his unborn child—spilled over to the young people of his community.

The regionals taught them a lot. Their chairs were too heavy. They had the strength of racers but not the finesse. They had a lot to learn about pacing themselves. But they still won enough points to compete in the nationals at New York City in mid-July.

Jan and Bonnie came with them, and they spent two days playing tourist: seeing New York from the top of the Empire State Building, taking in Fifth Avenue and Times Square, applauding the Fifth Dimension at the Waldorf Astoria, and going back again and again to Mama Leone's, an Italian restaurant with a tomato sauce they couldn't believe.

At the meet the competition was tough. Mike placed third in the 100-yard dash and felt lucky to get that. He came in second in the javelin throw. Curt felt disappointed in his own performance; but at the end of the meet, they learned that they had both earned enough points to send them to the Para-Olympics in Canada in August.

Back home in Utah, a "Send Mike and Curt to the Olympics" campaign began. The media widely featured the two and the needed money began to come in from businesses and townspeople, organizations and families, church and school groups. After years of being marginal members in some ways, Mike and Curt felt they could return the gift of belonging to a community by representing it at an international event.

The Olympic Village in August was beautiful. Their Canadian hosts were warm and friendly. At Etobico, the Toronto suburb where the Olympics would be held, the air was electric with anticipation and band music. The teams wheeled onto the huge track in alphabetical order, proud Canadian hosts carrying each country's flag. The music was almost drowned out by the ovations of the thousands of standing, cheering spectators. Mike felt chills running up and down his spine, and the lump in his throat threatened to choke him. Curt flashed him the ear-to-ear Brinkman grin that was his trademark and yelled, "Hey, whaddaya think of this, Johnson?" Mike could only nod.

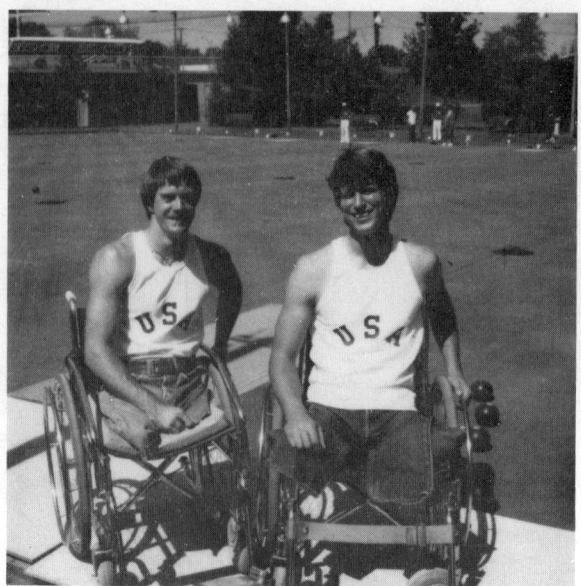

Lawnbowling with Curt Brinkman at the
1976 Para-Olympics

That night Mike couldn't sleep. Scenes of Vietnam came back. The jungle, the mine, seeing his mangled hands and shattered legs, the curtain of blood from his forehead sweeping down over his eyes. He thrashed restlessly, then replaced it with a vision of Jan's face. The steady light in her eyes, the warmth of her smile relaxed him and he drifted off to sleep.

The first event the next day was lawn bowling at a swank country club. The grass was brilliant green, precision manicured, and glistening. The crowds were welcoming and polite but proper. Curt and Mike were, through some fluke, pitted against each other for the first game. The officials' politeness did not waver when the two boys from Utah explained that they'd never seen the game before. Well, the object was to place your many "bowls," or wooden balls weighted on one side, as close as possible to a previously thrown white ball, a little larger than the cue ball in pool.

Mike got the feel of it rapidly and won 18-0. Curt grinned and threatened, "Watch out for the 100 meters!"

Mike beat his next two opponents easily, one from India and the other from Iran. He was now in the finals and would play the South African champion, Deon Huddlestone, for the gold after lunch.

As Mike chewed on the last of his sandwich, he spotted an amputee sitting in his chair under a big tree talking to someone. It had to be Deon and his manager. Mike wheeled over and introduced himself.

"Very nice to meet you, Mike," said Deon with a wide grin and a firm handshake. "Been watching you perform this morning. Very admirable. Where did you learn to play so well?"

Mike gave Deon a surprised look. "Well, uh, right here. This is the first time I've ever played."

Deon stared at Mike in silent disbelief. His manager asked incredulously, "Surely you're jesting, Mr. Johnson. A person can't begin as a complete novice and bowl the way you do."

"I'm not kidding, honest," Mike protested. "I've never even seen the game before."

The manager left shaking his head, and Deon and Mike talked about the game. Deon willingly gave Mike pointers on his play and the fine points of the game. Mike soaked it all up. Then he went back to the green to practice.

A bald and winking little old man appeared out of nowhere. Mike had seen him that morning, and he had given Mike some quiet pointers during the early play.

"Mr. Johnson? I believe you can beat our South African friend, and I would deem it an honor to have you use my bowls." He handed Mike a gleaming set of hand-polished wooden balls. "I would be very pleased to act as your manager, if you would have me."

Mike accepted on the spot, fondling the beautiful wood and listening as the little man outlined one strategy after another. Mike was grinning widely and nodding vigorously as his "manager" finished. He could hardly wait.

The championship match began before stands filled with patrons clad in white. It was the most subdued crowd Mike had ever performed before, but very attentive. Each well-placed bowl received a round of applause. Deon took an early 5-to-1 lead and seemed to be in excellent form until Mike switched strategy and began firing his bowls like rockets aimed at Deon's precisely placed bowls. While they were scattered royally, Mike began placing his own in strategic counting positions and soon had the South African tied 7 to 7.

Deon couldn't adjust to this new style of play and Mike, to his manager's delight, went on to beat the favored champion 18 to 7.

Mike was overwhelmed with joy and excitement. A gold medal!

Next day came the table-tennis competition. High from his medal in lawn bowling, Mike had supreme confidence, and he attacked the competition with gusto, slicing and backhanding his way to the semifinals. There he met a representative of the Egyptian team, a short guy balding in front. The Egyptian's offense was good, but he couldn't handle Mike's backhand slice return that curved as it came across the table. He could only return the ball by hitting it straight in the air, coming back to Mike high and deep. Each time, Mike took the invitation, smashing the ball back with powerful strokes, and caroming it off his opponent's forehead. After five repetitions of this bruising pattern, Mike had won the game.

The next day he faced off against Deon Huddlestone in the finals. He was determined to beat him, stunned that he had done so well, and keyed up for the match, living off the adrenaline and loving it.

The two young men were evenly matched, trading slices, backhands, and power hits. Each used every trick he knew, the volleys becoming longer and faster. Mike squeaked by Deon in the first game, and Deon took him in the second. As the crucial third set began, Mike took several deep breaths to relax himself. The U.S. team was on hand to cheer for Mike, and the South African team was equally noisy on Deon's side. Unexpected support came from the Egyptian team, which ranked itself solidly behind Mike. The lead seesawed back and forth, tension mounting, until Mike finally broke through to win with the required two points. Pandemonium erupted, the Egyptian team screaming, "USA! USA!" Mike's heart was hammering with pride.

He had received his lawn-bowling medal with a polite handshake and congratulations in the center of the green, but here it was the full ceremony. The American bronze medalist wheeled his chair up the lowest ramp, with the American flag fluttering behind him and the strains of the Para-Olympiad song in the air. Then Deon mounted the next ramp for the silver. As Mike wheeled to the top of the highest ramp and lowered his head for the medal, he saw the Stars and Stripes

Gold medalist in the table-tennis competition

rise. The band broke into "The Star-Spangled Banner." It was almost too much. With his hand over his heart and tears streaming down his face, he knew that the nightmare of Vietnam would come again but that he had this moment to efface it.

The next day Mike had no competition, so he wandered around watching the others. He stayed a long time at the quadraplegic events, for those paralyzed from the shoulders down. He cheered and whooped as the winners inched out ahead of the others, but in between times his face was sober, his eyes misty. Each move was agonizing for the competitors. Some could only flex an elbow thirty degrees and had to push off with the heel of their palms. Some had fingers too bent to use, so they had little spokes on the rims of their chairs that they could catch with the palm of their hand. At the end of each race, the winner crossed the finish line, turned, and waited for the others to finish, embracing each one as they wheeled across. Mike wept.

He watched blind kids do the long jump, pacing off the distance to their take-off line and then hitting it with amazing accuracy. He thought of leaping into the air blind, and shuddered. He wondered again if he'd have the courage to run flat out with only the voice of a caller to guide him, as they did in the 50- and 100-meter dashes. He responded to their aggressiveness and competition—their winning spirit. That night he was a little quieter than usual during the horseplay among members of the USA team.

When things had at last calmed down Mike lay quietly, thinking over what had happened. He vowed he would never feel sorry for himself again. He was in great shape compared to a lot of these kids. And he should be able to do better. He took a deep breath and faced up to something he'd been putting off since hospital days. Drugs. It had been six years since he'd tried to sleep without drugs. Even in top physical condition, trained to a fine competitive edge as he was, he still was taking Dalmane and Restoril each night to sleep. He didn't know when, but he knew that at some point his future would be drug-free.

The next day, Sunday, Mike went with two friends from BYU and spoke at a sacrament meeting. He loved it, but returned to an uneasy feeling that Curt and the rest of his competition were more prepared than he for the 100-meter dash. Curt had been practicing stops and starts in his borrowed racing chair. Mike hadn't even sat in his own yet. As he drifted off to sleep, he tried to figure out how much longer a hundred meters was than a hundred yards, but the math overwhelmed him.

When they lined up the next morning, Mike glanced to his left at Curt and at Deon on his right. Both of them looked focused, intense. Suddenly Mike's carefree casualness dropped away. This was a big race. He had to win it. Mike had the power for a great racing start and shot away when the starter's pistol barked, but Curt was ahead of him, his face a mask of determination. At twenty yards Deon was to Mike's left and starting to fall behind. The others were trailing. It was time to close in on Curt and sprint ahead. Mike poured on the power. Then more. He was giving it all he had, and Curt, running a beautiful race, was still wheeling ahead of him. Suddenly it was over. Mike was dumbfounded, even as he hugged his buddy and panted congratulations. He rolled away shaking his head, mad at himself for not preparing as much as he should have.

Mike's last event was the javelin, and his already shaken confidence wavered a bit more as he saw some of the fantastic

A borrowed javelin wins a bronze medal

practice throws made by other competitors. He approached a Swedish thrower and, gesturing, asked in broken English, "I use javelin? Your javelin? Give it back after?"

"Sure," the Swede grinned. "No big deal. Go right ahead."

Mike turned beet red and felt like an idiot.

When the competition began, Jerome of the USA threw first, his javelin soaring almost out of sight. Mike groaned. "I couldn't touch that toss if I shot it out of a gun!" Behan threw next, but not so far. Did Mike have a chance of beating him? Each contender took his turn. Mike kept score mentally. After six throws each, the three longest throws belonged to Jerome, Behan, and Mike's Swedish friend. Mike had one more throw, and it had to be perfect.

He took a deep breath and blew it out, concentrating, feeling everything inside him focus and sharpen. He arched back and let the javelin fly. It curved beautifully, not too high, and sailed out toward the Swede's marker. Mike held his breath. It fell point first. It was close, too close. He couldn't tell which was first. His heart pounded as he watched the officials hurry over to mark the point of impact. Mike read the figures with relief, breaking into a huge grin. He had beaten the Swede by four inches with the Swede's own javelin.

Two golds, a silver, and a bronze. He was an Olympian. And he'd be ready for Russia in 1980.

10

The Big Year

They sat on the couch for a long time, holding each other close. Television and newspaper reporters, crowds of well-wishers—it was fun and exciting but short-lived. Jan was forever. He had gone over every detail of the Olympic games, but Jan couldn't seem to get enough of it. Now they were just enjoying being close and alone, as if no one else existed. Every once in a while Jan would jump and groan, their baby reminding them with a well-placed kick that they were not completely alone.

In bed later Jan stirred, unable to sleep because of an unusual ache in her lower back. Strange how she had gone to bed feeling fine, couldn't remember straining her back that day, and now to be awakened by the nagging pain which seemed to radiate around to the front then slowly disappear, only to come back again. She looked out into the warm, clear October night and caught the distant, shadowy outline of the mountains. The fall season in Utah was a genuinely aesthetic experience; she loved it. Now the approaching pain brought her brain back to her body. She sank into an easy chair and placed a hand on her swollen abdomen. Only then did it hit her.

"Hey, I think I'm in labor. I think the baby's coming!" Jan sat timing the pains, excited and scared at the same time. She woke Mike reluctantly. He had so few nights of regular, relaxed sleep. "Mike. Mike, honey. Wake up. I think we're going to have a baby."

Mike jerked up suddenly, as though he were dreaming about 'Nam and the enemy were attacking. He rubbed his eyes with the back of one hand and fired off, "What's goin' on?" Jan laughed. Mike seemed too comical in his present state.

Seth was born at 7:10 A.M., Sunday, 10 October 1976, and they fell in love with him immediately. With his birth, something clicked for Mike. He felt like a family again. He had never felt closer to his own parents, closer to Jan.

The weeks passed rapidly for them. Mike worked doggedly at his psychology classes, but really came alive on the basketball court. He was the sparkplug of the team and sometimes felt that he was fanning a lonely flame. Many of the guys were in lousy shape, smokers with no real desire to work out and get in shape. They partied it up on the trips and put in their time on the court without sharing Mike's throbbing need to win. He was double-guarded regularly, but he was still the high point man for his team.

Then in late March 1977 came an invitation to play on the national all-star team. Selected wheelchair players rolled into Denver from Chicago, Florida, Kentucky, Indiana, Kansas, and California. He was stunned at a couple of huge black players, six feet nine inches tall, with powerful muscles except for the crippled foot or leg that kept them out of regular basketball. David Kiley, considered the best all-round player in the country, was matched up against Mike.

It was heaven for Mike. He was playing with a savvy team who could sense what he was going to do before he did it. Mike was bursting for action and had a chance to try all of the tricky moves that he'd never had a crack at before. The euphoria would take days to dissipate.

"Hey, Johnson." It was the big black center from Indiana. "You're good, man. You ought to play for the U.S. team." Mike considered, then approached one of the coaches.

"Hey, coach. I sure would love to play on your national team. Have I got the tools to make it?"

The coach looked at Mike silently, then said, "Mike, you're good. I'd love to have you on our team; you'd be a real strength. But you're an amputee."

Mike was shocked. "Well, that sure qualifies me to ride a wheelchair. I'm not reading you."

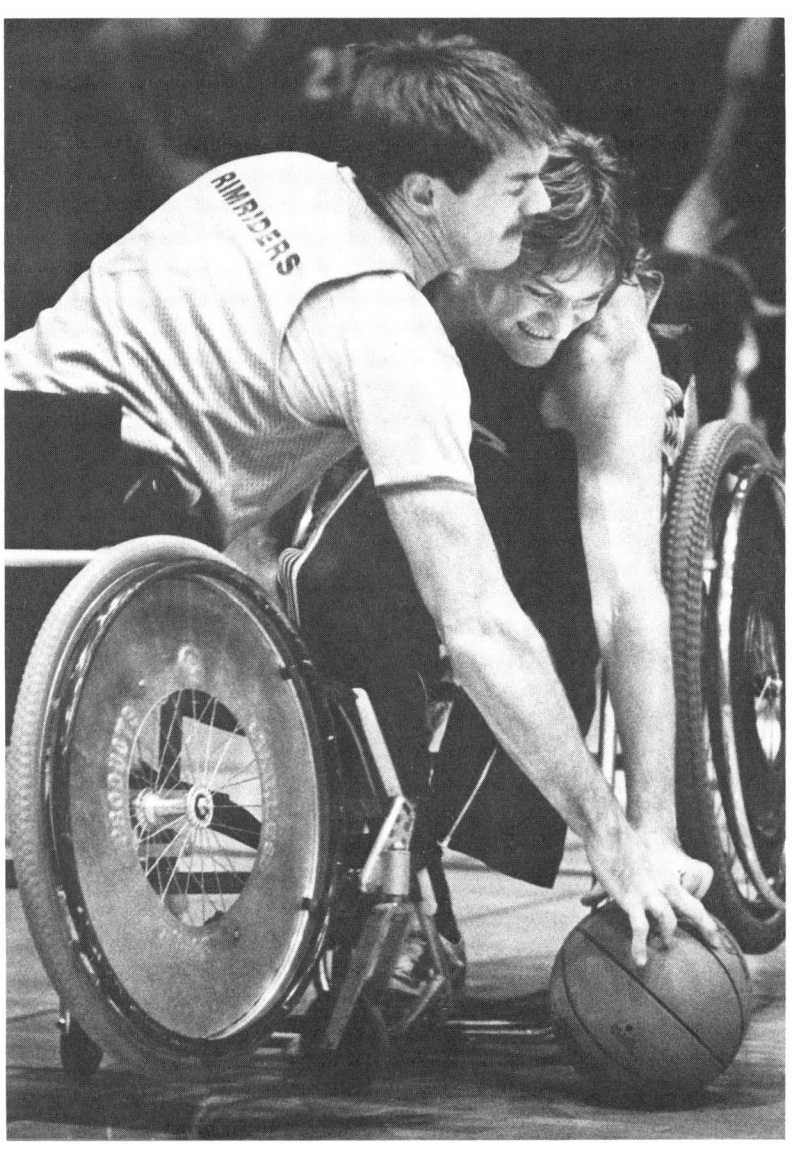
Battling for the ball against Ogden Spokemaster Jim Peterson
(Steve Jones — Ogden *Standard–Examiner*)

The coach drew a deep breath. "Well, Mike, the international tournaments like the Pan-American Games and the Stoke-Manville Games in England won't allow amputees on the squad." Mike was furious. He barely listened to the coach's explanation that Guggenheim, boss of the International Wheelchair Athletics Association, had outlawed amputees. He felt they had an advantage. Mike didn't buy it. He was lighter, easier to move, easier to knock off balance. If anything, that was a handicap. He left Denver angry!

The spring of 1977 was beautiful in many ways for Mike. He loved the season that nature reawakened and spent a lot of time with Jan and little Seth picnicking in the Wasatch Mountains that he so dearly loved. His university studies were still there, but Mike had a hard time getting very serious about school. The classroom confined him and just wasn't his favorite place. But he was excited about a new major—health sciences. His new goal professionally was to teach health and to coach, possibly basketball. He would see what the future brought.

But the near future smelled of track and field, and that caused Mike's blood to run fast. He and Curt had already started the workouts, hard, purposeful. Being outside on the track, seeing the huge, bold mountains jutting up into the clear, sharp Utah sky was magic to Mike's spirit. Training went well. Soon he was off to Denver for the 1977 Rocky Mountain Regional Wheelchair Games.

The first event in Denver was the javelin throw. Mike's new system of hooking his left arm around the handle on the back of his wheelchair and throwing over the back of the chair was producing tremendous results. At the line he eyed the field. The weather was perfect, the spotters out about seventy feet. The field record was sixty-seven feet, but Mike was sure he could pass that. Should he tell them to back up? No, he shook his head wryly. "They'll just think I'm a big show-off."

He concentrated, arched back, and fired the shaft into the air. The javelin sailed, swooshing over the spotters, who stared at it in utter disbelief. Mike set a new national record of eighty-seven feet, eleven and one-half inches.

The next event was the 100-yard dash. Mike had run away with a time of twenty-one seconds the year before. But this year the Californians had come, including Dawson, a fast

The Big Year

Setting a national record for the 100-yard dash, 1977

black kid. Mike heard someone whisper that a guy from Illinois was there, the fastest man wheelchair track had ever seen.

"Oh, great!" Mike moaned. "I could have gone all day without hearing that."

The starter called the competitors to the line. Mike was nervous, tense. He wanted this race and he was ready for it. He studied the starter, watching his moves, listening to his cadence. The forward leap of his wheelchair matched the starter's pistol perfectly. Mike's eyes and every atom of his body were concentrated on the finish tape. It was over and Jan was jumping up and down yelling, "You won, Mike! You won! You wiped them! There was no one even close." It was another new national record: 17.5 seconds, beating the old record of 18.6 seconds by 1.1 second.

Mike wheeled over to watch Curt in the class five 100-yard dash. Could he match Mike's time? When the gun went off, Curt shot to the front and stormed down the track, winning easily. He came in at 17.6, one tenth of a second later than Mike's. Mike grinned, yelled out his congratulations, and went on to his next event, while Curt nodded back, clearly disappointed.

Mike went on to win five gold medals, an unprecedented feat in a national track-and-field meet.

As Mike and Jan showed up at the awards banquet on the last evening, Mike was feeling good. He had broken two national records, had swept his events with five gold medals. He should be the top contender for the prestigious Outstanding Athlete award. He grinned at Jan, but she held his hand hard. She knew how tense he was.

Then came the announcement: "As Outstanding Athlete, Curt Brinkman." Mike's mouth dropped open. Curt had set a new record in the mile, and it had been the deciding factor. He congratulated Curt exuberantly, but it was his turn to feel disappointed.

The summer disappeared in a flurry of training, traveling, and meets. Mike and Curt both did very well in San Diego in early June. Then it was time for the national finals in San José in late June. This time Jan couldn't go, but Cathy, her sister in San José, was there to cheer Mike on. He did well, placing in several events, but it was the slalom he really wanted. He pointed out the hard part to Cathy over the roars of the crowd. "See the bridge, that trestle made up of four-by-fours? That's the tough part. If you fall off the rails, you can go right through. If you come off the side, you're disqualified because you've touched the floor." He laughed. "From that height, you can really crash and burn. Oh man, I get fired up just looking at it!"

Cathy stared at the course in disbelief, gave Mike a good luck kiss, and went to the sidelines.

Mike waved good-bye and moved up closer to the slalom. He yelled "howdy" to Jim Osborn, the originator of the California slalom. Jim was finishing his set-up by placing the wooden squares with little flags in strategic places. Mike made mental notes of locations. Each flag touched added a second to a participant's time. Since most of the guys hit several, a clean run would win it. Mike was going to make a clean run, he could feel it. This was his baby. He owned it.

The class threes were finished now and the meet officials began calling class four names, telling the participants how to line up. He wanted his hands as sweaty and sticky as possible. Time and again, Mike picked up the wet towel in his lap and ran it over his rims, his wheels, to keep them as clean as possible. He was getting psyched. He was fast and strong, in excellent shape. He licked the salt from his lips. This was his year.

Mike watched his competitors and their times as he continued to pump up and down the corridor. The front wheels of the chair broke an electronic tape which triggered a computerized clock. The clock was up high, in full view of the crowd, and they went wild as the wheelers raced through the barrage of obstacles. Mike watched as contestants knocked funnels down, backed up into flags, got them in their spokes, even fell off the bridge.

By the entrance to the slalom, waiting their turn, were the two Californians, David Agular and Manny Via. They practiced constantly on the permanent slalom at Whitney High School close to their home. They looked at Mike with broad grins and waved in unison. Mike waved back, grinning just as broadly. He knew they were there to beat him. Well, he wouldn't let them. But they were awfully good.

Six were left now. Mike was talking to himself, psyching himself up. "Okay, Johnson, you've got only one crack at the slalom. It's a one-time shot. You goof up and you're gone. Nope. I gotta be good. This is my event."

Mike zeroed his concentration in on the starter. The guy counted cadence, then fired, but the gun didn't start the clock. The front wheels of the chair hitting the tape did. Now Mike knew how to get the edge. He watched the finish line. Breaking the tape there stopped the clock. Another plan formed in his mind. He went to the starting line anxious and ready.

"You ready, Johnson?" the starter asked.

Mike nodded. "I'm ready." Mike's tension pushed his voice up a notch.

"Well, then move up to the starting line."

Mike's front wheels were fully three feet behind the line. "I'd like to start back here if it's not illegal."

The starter looked puzzled, then illuminated. "Nope, it's not illegal. On your mark," he barked. "Get set . . ." Blam! Mike's chair shot forward, picking up valuable speed as he broke through the tape, starting the clock.

Mike zoomed in to the zigzag formation, flying into a chute forward, then turning around and coming out backwards. He did ten of them in rapid succession, then dashed down the

Setting a national record in the California slalom, 1977

straightaway into a parking area. The huge crowd, first hushed, now was clapping and cheering. As Mike reached the bridge without touching a single flag, the crowd began to roar. He powered down the bridge ramp, whirled around the corner. After two fast back-ups, Mike flipped a smooth, flowing U-turn, then blazed down the chute into the tape, leaning out over his front wheels to make sure the tape was broken. The crowd was roaring their approval. Mike saw people glance at the clock, then freeze increduously, then erupt in shouting and clapping. The deafening applause went on and on. Mike, feeling flushed and sweaty with a tired exuberance, was accepting congratulations from competitors when the announcer broke through the noise.

"Michael Johnson of Provo, Utah, has just set a new national record in the slalom event with a time of one minute and fifty-seven seconds." The roar of the crowd drowned him out.

Cathy was crying and hugging him, babbling almost incoherently. "Mike, you nut, you were fantastic. I've never seen anything like it! You were almost fifteen seconds ahead of the guy in second place. Mike, I—I just can't believe it. Oh, I wish Jan were here."

Jim Osborn presented the medal. "Ladies and gentlemen," his voice boomed through the mike. "This is the reason I designed the slalom."

11

"The Dumbest Thing!"

"Curt, you have to be crazy! I'm ready to try most things, but this is the dumbest thing I've ever heard of!"

Curt flashed that Brinkman ear-to-ear grin. "Look, Johnson, it'll be the greatest way in the world to raise money for the Handicapped Van."

Mike eyed him warily. It was July 1977 and Utah County Handicapped Awareness had been working hard trying to raise money for a van that would transport the handicapped. "I dunno, Curt. The farthest I've gone is twenty-five miles. What are you talking—over a hundred?"

Curt nodded, "Yeah, 115. But it'll hit the record books. Should get a lot of publicity."

Mike shook his head. "I still think you're nuts, Brinkman—but I'll do it with you."

That's how they decided to make a run from Provo, around Utah Lake, and back to Utah Lake State Park near the Geneva Steel Plant in Orem, in late August.

They started at K-96 Radio in Provo in the early hours of an August morning. Hours later, when they reached the little village of Palmyra, they were met by a Mormon bishop and his family who presented them with the money his ward had raised. Just before they got to Genola, they came across a young rattlesnake that kept striking at the wheels.

By the time the sun had climbed into a scorching position, they had done all of thirty miles.

They stopped for a rest and a salt tablet, and everyone in

The trek around Utah Lake with Curt Brinkman, August 1977
(courtesy of the *Daily Herald*, Provo, Utah)

the van started telling them they had done enough. "Come on, Mike," Jan said. "Eighty-five miles left and look at you. Nobody will blame you if you quit now. Look what you've done already!"

They kept going! The west side of the lake seemed all uphill, and the wind was blowing against them. The sun beat down straight out of the script for a desert movie; and just when they thought maybe they weren't going to make it, the rain came. It wet the rims, which was uncomfortable; but the rain was so cool and such a break from the glaring sun, it gave them new life.

Near Lehi, a group of joggers joined them. Then more and more people joined in, so that by the time they wheeled by the Geneva Steel Plant, there was a huge crowd of people waving, honking, and cheering. Even so, those last few miles were an agony.

Curt's hands, arms, and buttocks were numb, and he was getting awful pains in his back. "My lower back was just killing me from pushing forward and coming down and back up and down, then back up," he said later. "I was so stiff and sore that I couldn't sit up straight. It was incredible. The part that got me the worst was in the wrists and fingers. They're not built to work like ankles and feet, so the tendons and muscles were really overworked. It just wiped me out royal!"

Mike also described the trauma of those last few miles. "I wasn't so sure that I could really finish. The last stretch was agony—it was horrible. I was so sore from bending over, leaning over, and pushing my chair through the rain and wind that my back just about fused in one position. I would then look up and try to straighten my back and scream from the pain."

Jan cried, begging them to quit, but something in him wouldn't. At approximately 11:00 P.M. in darkness made into dusk by the headlights of many cars, two wheelchairs rolled across the finish line. They had done it, one hundred and fifteen miles in seventeen hours! The world record up to that point had been one hundred and eight miles in five days.

That fall, Brigham Young University honored the two wheelers as exemplary young men and invited them to light the torch at the top of the large block Y. The event, staged during the Homecoming events at a BYU football game, was a double honor for Mike and Curt because they were the first students ever invited to light the Y. The afternoon was gorgeous, full of warmth and color and dignitaries. But for Mike, it was in a class by itself for him to be recognized as an outstanding athlete by his own school.

12

New Loves, New Lessons

Mike opened his eyes and then lay there looking out of the window into the steel gray of the early October morning, wondering why he was awake. He felt for Jan. She was gone. He heard her stirring in the kitchen.

"What's up?" Mike frog-leaped across the living room carpet and jumped up into a padded kitchen chair. Jan was making orange juice.

"I'm not sure. But I have these pains—almost like labor pains." She wrapped her fingers around her swollen abdomen.

"Janny, the baby is still two months away. I mean, the baby can't be coming, could it?"

Her face looked as puzzled as his. "Oh, Mike, I just don't know. It almost feels like the baby has dropped some, and the pains are real and regular. I think we had better get it checked out."

Matthew came later that afternoon, 9 October 1977. It was a difficult birth. Mike couldn't understand why such a tiny wrinkled baby had such a tough time coming. During the next few days Mike and Jan sat for hours in the special intensive care unit for newborns—waiting, wondering, talking in low tones with other parents whose babies lay in the little lighted compartments. Mike couldn't see how the baby could survive. His minute body was a maze of tubes and wires. But he was a fighter. Four weeks later the Johnsons took their new baby home.

New Loves, New Lessons

Mike's bishop asked him to coach an Explorer basketball team in their ward that winter. The team had lots of desire, Mike told Jan ruefully, but zero talent. He brought his boys along slowly, stressing the fundamentals. They lost their first games; but as the season progressed, Mike's team became a scrappy, hard-playing unit. Everyone came to practice and to the games. Mike allowed no yelling, hollering, and complaining; that was his job. He was the coach; they were the players. If they got a bad call against them, it was Mike's fight with the refs, not theirs. Negative comments or arguing brought them out of the game fast, giving them plenty of time to sit on the bench and think. The young men knew where they stood with Mike, what he expected from them. The discipline paid off. Alpine made it to the regional finals.

The final game was played in Provo. Mike nervously rolled his wheelchair back and forth in the dressing room, glancing at the determined, questioning faces all focused on him.

"Coach." One of the boys broke the silence. "This is a tough team. I mean, they got Sylvester. He's as big as his brother, the Olympic discus champion. You think we can beat them?"

Mike wouldn't lie to them. He chose his words carefully. "We've come a long way together. I've watched you improve tremendously. We've worked hard. We deserve to be here tonight, and we deserve to go to the finals in Salt Lake City. We *will* be in the Salt Lake finals because we're winners. Sure, Sylvester's tough, but he's only one player. He can only do so much. Let's go out there and play our game, take it to them, run them to death. If you screw up, miss a shot, don't sweat it. Get back in the game. Don't be looking over at me unless I yell to you. Stay with your man, go for the fast breaks, work the ball, take the good shots."

Mike sucked in his breath, paused for a moment, then concluded: "Boys, I'm awfully proud of you no matter what happens tonight. You're all fantastic young men. We'll say our prayer. Then let's go play a ball game." The young jersey-clad players crowded around Mike's chair and bowed their heads.

The game was fast. More than once Mike disagreed vehemently with the referee on calls but always stopped short of getting a technical foul. Mike didn't want to penalize his boys. It was like a chess game. What his team lacked in skill, they were making up in tenacity. But early in the fourth quarter the

Provo team began to break into the lead. By the time Mike could call a timeout, Alpine was behind by ten points.

Mike looked down at the five exhausted players drenched in sweat sitting on the floor. What could he tell them about reaching down and coming up with the victory? He had done it himself. But how could he put it in words?

"Guys, you're playing a heck of a game. There're only a few minutes left. After the game you can rest for a long time, but right now we've got a game to win. We've worked hard. We have weeks of hard work invested in this game. Now let's use our investment. This is how we are going to win this game."

Mike quickly made some adjustments and outlined a strategy. The shrill whistle called his players back onto the floor. The Provo team had the ball. Suddenly the boys from Alpine attacked with a tight press, collapsing on the ball. The Provo team panicked, one of their players throwing a wild pass right to an Alpine player. He quickly turned and threw a baseball pass to a teammate who went in for an easy two. The press and trap worked again and again, the score coming closer. But with seconds left, the Provo team was still one point ahead.

Mike's boys brought the ball down the court. They worked the ball patiently. Six seconds, five, four, three. The crowd was screaming. "Shoot! Shoot!" The ball flew to the player at the side of the key. Determined and confident, he leaped straight and high, wrapped his hands around the ball over his head, then spun the ball off his fingers in a high overhead arch. The crowd was silent. The ball seemed to hang in the air, then swished cleanly through the net.

The Alpine crowd went wild. The evening ended with a victory feast at McDonald's. The team concluded the season by winning third place in the all-Church finals. And Mike had found a new love.

Mike found it harder to start training in that spring of 1978, even though he had received a letter informing him that amputees were now eligible for that year's Pan-American games. In the regional games Mike barely missed winning the 100-yard dash again, though he won both the slalom and the javelin. The narrow miss disgusted him and he settled down to hard training. He was determined to win in the national games in Virginia.

Training for *Deseret News* Marathon, 1978

Mike began the nationals with wins in the slalom and the javelin. Then it was time for the 100-yard race again. Mike broke the national record in an early heat. Jan found a good spot and checked her movie camera before the final heat. She wanted this race on film, for the kids, for everyone. She was sure he could win this time. Mike was at the line. Among the competitors was the man who had beat him in California, all fast starters. Mike knew he had to do something to shake things up. He was right in the middle of the pack. He watched the starter, leaning forward on the first command, then stroked hard just before the starter pulled his trigger. It was a false start. Another and he would be out of the race.

"Got the jitters, Johnson?" Others fired similar comments at Mike as they lined up once again. Mike hoped this would give him an edge, get the others distracted.

This time he waited until the starter squeezed the trigger. Mike made a perfect start. Jan, with her trigger finger trembling, followed Mike with the humming movie camera down the track. He was way ahead of everyone else and still gaining ground. Then it was over. Mike knew he had won the race in

In front nearing finish line of 100-yard dash, Virginia, 1978

the sixteen-second range. Maybe a new record? He coasted down the track, hands raised high in victory. After three years of trying, Mike had finally won the national 100 yards. Other competitors coasted past and reached out to shake Mike's hand, congratulate him.

"Mr. Johnson. You're disqualified." Mike swung around and stared. There was an official's flag pinned to the voice's shirt. The official began his speech again, his voice full of authority. "You're disqualified. You swerved into somebody else's lane and interfered with him. You're out."

Mike and Jan were speechless but Mike's shock passed quickly. He glared at the official.

"Interfered? I was a full seven or eight yards ahead. How could I have interfered with anyone? I crossed the finish line right on the edge of the tape in my lane, and I ran a straight race. I had to, to run such a fast race. I didn't swerve, man. You've got to be kidding. Maybe you mistook someone else for me." Mike was sweating now and shaking. He couldn't let this victory be taken from him.

The lane judge wouldn't reverse his decision. Mike stayed on the track, not letting them run another race until they solved this disastrous problem. The head judges stood behind the lane judge.

"It's not that big of a deal, Mike," one said, "there will be another year."

Mike ignored the 880 and returned to the dorm. He wouldn't talk to Jan. He didn't want his anger to spill over on her.

Three days later Mike had still not shaken the depression or the anger. He had finally won the 100-yard dash, and they had taken it from him. Mike wasn't chosen to be a member of the Pan-Am Team either.

"Sorry, Mike, I guess the problem with the 100-yard dash ruled against you," one of the coaches had said. Mike knew that remark translated into: We don't want a hothead representing the United States in Brazil.

Two weeks later he and Jan sat in their basement to watch the newly developed film of the race. They watched the film several times, backed it up and replayed crucial seconds, slowed down the speed. There was no justification for his disqualification. Mike was angry all over again.

He knew he had to let go of the anger. In late summer Mike took a trip to the desert. It was dark when he reached Death Canyon. The clouds blocked out any light from the moon. It was a little spooky, but in a delicious way.

"Oh, Johnson, you're so brave," Mike exclaimed to himself in the dark of the truck cab. "Louis L'Amour would be proud of you."

With that little speech, Mike dropped his equipment from the door and followed it into the sand. He pitched the tent and lit a campfire. Feeling very alone, he thought and wrote in his journal well into the night. Mike mentally went back home to West Virginia, then back to Vietnam and his fight to survive in the hospitals. He thought about Casey. And then Jan and their two sons.

He pictured the strained face of the official at the race. Somehow Mike felt calmer now. He thought of how that official must have felt when he saw the pictures showing that his decision had been wrong. Mike could let go, forgive. That was the feeling he had come here to find. Sleep came easy—a deep, satisfying sleep.

Mike woke to the bawling of cows. He stuck his head out of the flap of the tent. Five cows, standing around a watering hole no more than twenty feet away, stared back at Mike.

Then the ultimate insult. He could also hear human voices. A truck and camper glinted on the hill above his camp. Clustered around the camper was a throng of people waving at him and yelling down greetings. They were probably collecting fossils. Mike waved back, then quickly ducked back into the tent. He felt foolish. He had been out here heroically alone, taming the West, conquering his fears. So much for Louis L'Amour.

Then Mike began to chuckle as he rolled up his sleeping bag. It felt good to laugh at himself. He needed more of that.

Three days later a tired yet content Mike pulled up in front of his home in Alpine.

Fall of 1978 came splashing into Utah with warmth and coziness, bathing the mountains in hues of oranges, golds, and deep reds. Some parts of the Wasatch Range were absolutely breathtaking, and Mike and Jan explored most of them. They fell in love again that fall, with a kick-back-and-relax attitude that lent easiness to their life-style. Hunting season brought a very uncommon pair into the woods, a double amputee in a wheelchair and his pregnant wife, puffing along with her excess load. But they had a great time. Mike was beginning to catch on to what too few people know; that the sweetness in life comes from simple, uncluttered love. It was there, and he was beginning to mellow, to become less intense and more content. It was a good change.

There were still frustrations, however. Mike couldn't do everything a husband with legs could, consequently Jan had to do extra household chores. She didn't seem to mind, but it bothered Mike. Then there was school. Mike liked the idea of teaching health education and coaching in high school, but going to classes and studying was a struggle. He stayed with it, however, and inched closer to graduation.

Winter brought wheelchair basketball and also little Rachel on 2 November. Mike sat beside her for a long time the first night they brought their daughter home.

Home was a place Mike was enjoying more and more. He loved coming home on cold winter afternoons. As he neared the door, he could hear little feet pounding across the kitchen floor and excited cries from two little boys. "Dad's home, Dad's

New Loves, New Lessons

A successful hunting trip

home." The door would inevitably fly open, and Seth would charge his dad, yelling "Dad's home" and "Did you bring me a prize?" Meanwhile, little Matthew would get to the stairs, turn around backwards, stretch out and swish down the stairs as if they were a chute, right into his dad's arms. Mike loved it—the same crazy experience every afternoon, and he loved every second of it. Home was Mike's favorite place to go. He wanted his children always to feel that way, too. Too many kids headed for the neighbors' because their own home was too uptight, too threatening.

He noticed that home seemed a little more hectic than before, though. One evening after Jan had bathed the boys, both of them came running out to where he was playing with Rachel, then just a few months old. He barely had time to put her in a safe place before they were all over him for their nightly romp. By the time Jan got the bathroom mopped up and came in, all of the cushions were off the couch and a basket of toys had been spilled. Everyone was shrieking wildly, including Rachel, who had rolled under the table, dislodging a stack of magazines.

Suddenly Jan was shrieking too. "Stop it! Stop it this minute!" She charged into the mess, eyes blazing. "Mike Johnson, this happens every night and then I have to spend an hour calming down the boys while you go play basketball." She scooped up Rachel. "All you ever do is have fun around here. Fun, fun fun! Who does the work? You take all your drugs at night and sleep in until noon every day. I need help, Mike." She was sobbing through her angry words and took Rachel off to the bedroom.

Mike glared speechlessly at her retracting back. "You're living off money from this person who only has fun!" he yelled. Jam slammed the door. Fuming, Mike swung out to his truck and went to basketball practice to work off his head of steam, but he couldn't shake Jan's comment on the drugs.

All during practice and on the way home Mike pondered his situation at home. He would not, could not experience another divorce. What was the problem, what was happening to him and Jan? He first tried to rationalize his position by feeling sorry about his mutilated body and Jan's lack of understanding. Then the seriousness of the situation caused Mike to be more honest in his consideration.

"Am I too selfish, do I expect Jan to do too much? Do I do enough for and give enough to her? Oh, I love that woman; I've got to make some changes. The sleep meds. Is that our big problem?"

Mike thought of his ritual of every evening, in fact of twelve years of nights. He had actually increased the sleep medication he used. By now it was a whole handful of Seconal and Percodan tablets. Mike tried to hide from Jan the amount he took, but that didn't make anything easier. Bedtime would begin with a book, something to eat, a little conversation, and then rapidly conclude as Mike passed out in mid-sentence, deep in weird chemical dreams, leaving Jan tense and unhappy. She knew Mike was in trouble. It was getting worse, and it would be noon tomorrow before he would be awake enough to make sense. Mike knew all this and knew it was the single biggest tension-causer in their marriage. He had tried to quit, but as soon as drug supplies were low, a jittery, uptight Mike sought out more prescriptions from yet another doctor. "I'll go camping, get out on the desert in the spring. Then I can lick it, I know I can." Deep down Mike knew he couldn't do it himself, he needed help. And he would get help sometime in the near future! With that thought the lights of the Jimmy flashed onto the driveway of the Johnson home.

He was ready to kiss and make up when he got home, but Jan was either asleep or pretending. The living room was still a mess and he started to straighten it up, then decided he'd do it in the morning when he wouldn't make so much noise.

Next morning he slept in and only gradually awakened to the sound of slamming doors and the simultaneous wailing of the three children.

So Jan was still mad and taking it out on the kids? He felt his anger flare up all over again. He dressed quickly and swung out. "Put my fishing stuff in the truck, will you, Jan?" he asked. "I'll be late getting home tonight."

She was changing diapers and, through the pins in her mouth, mumbled "Fine." It sounded as if she meant it.

He drove off thinking, "Maybe it's true. A few years of marriage and it's no fun anymore."

Jan was in bed reading when he got home that night. As he came out of the bathroom, he noticed that she was watching him with a surprised expression. He hoped it meant she was feeling a little calmer. He'd felt kind of guilty all day. Maybe the kids were getting her down. Maybe they needed to get away. Maybe he should help more. "What is it, Honey?" he asked, gently.

"You know, Mike," she responded with gentleness, "I just watched what you have to do to do something as simple as go to the bathroom, and it struck me that I've never heard you complain." He swung into bed beside her and she put out her arms to him. "I guess neither one of us is perfect, huh?"

He grinned, feeling an upsurge of relief as that dark shadow from his first failed marriage fell away. "Not yet, anyway. Except for you."

A picnic with sons Seth and Matt

A distinct change was occurring in Mike's life. Other people, family, friends, the kids in the neighborhood, were becoming much more important than before. Though athletics were still important, Mike was becoming aware that there were many avenues of his life he was just discovering.

The team jelled under the tutelage of Jeff Jonas, a pro basketball player. The season sped by with win after win. The players were stunned by their success. Mike's personal play was phenomenal. He would fake, swerve, go around to get free, then everything Mike threw up to the hoop went in. He was playing over his head. Mike threw up one shot as he fell out of his chair. The ball hit nothing but the bottom of the net!

Then the accident occurred. It was toward the end of the last game. The ball was on the floor, rolling slowly toward the out-of-bounds line. Mike and a Portland player closed in on the ball. Just as Mike reached down to scoop the ball up in his arm, the opposing player's chair rammed into Mike, its front footrest slicing into Mike's arm. The deep lacerations spurted bright red blood, which ran down Mike's arm and pooled on the hardwood. Quickly Mike was surrounded with helpers. Direct pressure placed over the gaping wound by a first aider slowed and then stopped the bleeding. While it was being bandaged, several suggested to Mike he leave the game and get stitches.

"Are you kidding. With six minutes left? No way, José. We're gonna win this game." With that, play resumed. Mike scored again and again, leaving a trail of blood wherever he went and all over the ball.

That winter, Mike's team won most of their games. Mike usually led in points. Soon the phone was ringing with calls from other teams trying to recruit him.

The successful season was good for Mike in many ways. It added to his confidence, his self-concept. But more important, it released Mike from a need to prove himself in wheelchair basketball. He had arrived as one of the best players in America, and he knew it. Would the drive still be there for track and field, especially after the Fisherville incident? Spring was fast approaching, and the strength of Mike's desire to prepare would answer the question.

One afternoon in early spring, Mike had just pulled in from school, feeling frustrated and uptight from flunking a test in a class he detested. Jan knew immediately he was upset and in her easy way soon had him talking out his feelings.

"Janny, am I ever going to graduate?"

Suddenly the phone interrupted the conversation. "Yes, Bishop, he's right here." Jan handed Mike the phone, shrugging her shoulders in a questioning way.

"Hi, Bishop Goeckeritz. What can I do for you?" A pause, then Mike soberly responded: "Okay, I'll be right over."

Even more soberly Mike returned an hour later. "The bishop asked me to be Scoutmaster of our ward troop."

Picture taken by a Scout at Boulder Mountain "superactivity" campout

Jan was smiling. "What did you tell him?"

His answer was slow in coming. "Well, I told him I would make a decision and let him know. I'm scared, Jan. I'm not prepared for a position like that. I don't know if I could handle it."

Mike talked about it and thought about it and prayed about it for three days. Then he told the bishop yes. When he took over he went immediately into high gear. He studied, took classes, organized, and was always doing something with the Scouts.

It was the basketball-team story all over again. Mike could pull the best out of these young men. He rewarded rank advancements and merit badges with campouts. The troop rarely went without everyone. That July Mike was the only adult to accompany his thirteen boys on a "superactivity" to Boulder Mountain in southern Utah.

It was a beautiful mountain, rising up out of the red, dusty desert like an oasis. The boys loved the rough climb from the desert floor up into the green coolness of the high pines and firs. For days they camped, hiked, fished, played. At nights, with hazy campfire smoke curling into the lights above, Mike and his boys shared stories, songs, ideas, then knelt and prayed their thankfulness to the God who had created this wonderland.

Some of the Scouts had had doubts about a Scoutmaster without legs. How could he get around on a trip as rugged as this? In the end, after they watched Mike wheel, drive, hop up the trail on his hands, and go anywhere the Scouts could go, they were all believers. Mike became, not a Scoutmaster without legs, but a Scoutmaster, a leader to be looked up to. The fact that Mike didn't have legs got lost unless the boys consciously thought about it.

Each glorious, sunlit day began with Old Glory and the troop flag being raised high on the huge flagpole, two tall straight pines lashed together. An amazing thing occurred with those flags. Each morning, as the sun began its ascent, its first rays seemed to touch the flags, then as it dipped its head in sleepiness each dusk, it rallied behind the flags, its rays slowly dimming and giving way to lengthening shadows. At night the flags would be lowered in a special ceremony. Mike felt strongly about the flag and wanted his Scouts to know he was one vet who loved his flag and his country. When Mike returned home, he entered in his journal: "One of the truly great experiences of my life. I don't just like this Scouting job, I love it. It's so easy to love these boys."

13

A Different Treasure

That fall and winter Mike worked hard in school. A successful school year would mean graduation in April of 1979. Mike wanted that for Jan as much as for himself. Jan had been very patient with Mike's career struggle, but even her patience was starting to wear a bit thin. Wheelchair basketball still competed for Mike's time that winter, but it was no longer alone on center stage.

During the spring Mike spent as much time gardening as training for summer track events. He had tenaciously battled with the VA and won a small garden tractor.

Early April was soon for gardening, but the soil warmed by the early spring sun beckoned and Mike couldn't resist. He sat right down in the churned-up dirt, feeling it, smelling it. A honk brought Mike out of his agrarian trance. He waved to the mailman and wheeled over to the mailbox. The long white envelope, very official, had come from the Olympics committee.

Jan stood at the door, balancing a squirming Rachel on her hip. They read the letter together. It was Mike's official invitation to compete in the Olympics in Holland. His events would be the 100-meter race and the 1500-meter relay, lawn bowling, javelin, and table tennis.

Jan's eyes sparkled. "Oh, Mike, I'm so proud of you. Holland! Maybe you can bring me home some tulips!"

A Different Treasure

Clearing snow on his new tractor

Mike smiled. He was looking at the bottom of the letter. "Hey, Jan, this is signed by Ben Lipton. He's the head man of wheelchair track and field."

Jan looked down at the letter. "Are you excited?"

Mike snorted, "Is the Pope Catholic? 'Course I'm excited. But I've really got to get movin', get training." The next morning Mike was wheeling down the road toward the mountain, his mountain. He would be ready, especially for the 100 meters.

"Mike, you're wanted on the phone. It's long distance from California. Can you hear me?" Jan was yelling as loud as she could and still wasn't sure Mike could hear her over the roar of the tractor engine. But the noise stopped, and Mike dropped down from the machine.

"Yeah, this is Mike Johnson." He listened for a long time. Jan watched Mike's forehead pucker. Something about Scouting?

"Well, Brother Gould, as I said, that's the same week as the Olympics, but maybe I can work something out. Thanks for the opportunity. I sure would love to come. I'll make a decision and let you know in a few days. Okay, thanks. 'Bye." He hung up slowly.

Mike sat there with a dazed look on his face. Jan couldn't stand it any longer.

"Mike, for heaven's sake, what was that all about? Who was it?"

"Well, heck, Jan. I've got a problem. This is gonna be a tough one." Mike hesitated, staring out of the window.

"Michael, will you please tell me what that phone call was all about!"

Mike fumbled it out. Jay Gould, Church leader and Scouter from Sacramento, California, had read about Mike and had invited him to be a principal speaker at the LDS Boy Scouts' sesquicentennial campout in the High Sierras. This was a very significant event, with hundreds of Boy Scouts in attendance. It was a rare opportunity and a great honor, especially for someone who felt as Mike did about Scouting.

For a full week Mike weighed alternatives and continued to train. Mike could imagine standing in front of a cheering crowd in Holland, a gold medal about his neck as the band played the American national anthem and Old Glory fluttered up the pole. How could he give that up? On the other hand, how many young lives could he affect during three days living with and talking to over a thousand Scouts? He looked at the faces of his three children. What would he want them to know about him when they were the age of Scouts?

"On the other hand . . ." Mike chuckled to himself. He was now sounding just like old Tevye, the Russian Jew of *Fiddler on the Roof*. Mike had a sudden desire for isolation. He needed the desert again. The decision had to be made before it drove him and his family crazy.

Mike got in the truck and headed south past Delta, turning into the desert just past Hinckley. He could feel the heat of the June sun now. The summer sun had not yet burnt off the sparse grass, and the sagebrush was still tinted green. Mike loved the rugged, harsh beauty of the desert. And the silence, the isolation.

At last Mike pulled up in Death Canyon near Antelope Flats. Off to the southwest he could see Notch Peak. This time he would get away from the people and the cows. He stopped and made camp. Dusk was creeping in upon the desert, making mild shadows that lurked and stretched. The sunset was a dazzling display of oranges and lavenders and reds. Mike could easily see why this area was known as the Superstition Hills.

He threw a piece of pine onto the fire. A fire was like a friend out here alone on the desert. When he finally laid down his journal and snapped off the tape recorder, sleep came easily, healing, nourishing. There were no anxious moments in the night, no bad dreams set off by chemicals in his blood.

Three days were filled with exploring, looking, lying back and studying the sky. Introspection went deep: "Who are you, Mike Johnson? Where are you? What are you doing? Where are you heading? What's going on with you? Where do you want to be?" Finally the answer came, clear and solid and easy. Why had it been such a struggle?

The airport was crowded. It was seven o'clock on a Friday morning, and the weekend traveling had begun. Jan hustled Mike through the inspection station and down the long, wide corridor to the terminal. They were impervious to the usual stares at the guy with no legs breezing along in a wheelchair and a beautiful young woman running along beside him. There had been too many years of stares.

Mike and Jan held each other close. The people began to board Mike's flight. They traded last-minute instructions and then Jan looked confidently into Mike's eyes.

"I'm very proud of you for the decision you've made. You have so much you can share with those Boy Scouts. Winning a gold medal would be neat for you and me, but you have a chance to affect hundreds of lives in California. I know you'll do great."

Mike was met at the Sacramento Airport by Grant Gould, one of Jay Gould's seven children, who drove him up into the evergreen forest. Soon they could see the different Scout troops camped in clearings throughout the forest. As the pair approached the top of the last rise, Mike spotted a big teepee pitched next to a large natural amphitheater. Towering high above the amphitheater was a massive, rocky cliff. He wanted to crawl to the top of that cliff and look out over the mountain scene, but Jay was waiting in Mike's tent.

After introductions, Mike stowed his gear in one of the tents, changed into his heavy denim pants, pulled on his gloves, and wheeled his chair to the base of the rocky cliff.

"Well, Grant, my boy. I'm going to climb this baby. Want to come with me?"

Grant's eyes grew wide. He had been pushing this man around in his wheelchair and carrying things for him. "Do you really think you can? I mean, it's awfully steep and rocky, Mike. Have you climbed mountains before?"

Mike just grinned and sprang out of his chair, using his arms, and frog-leaped over to the first large boulder. He pulled his gloves snugly onto his fingers and began scrabbling up the mountain. Grant wasn't one to be left behind.

After a twenty-five-minute climb, the two hit a small ridge and then one final boulder that crowned the hill of rock. They pushed, pulled, and grunted to the top, then sat in silence gulping in the air and gazing at the breathtaking scene that lay below. Jutting above them was a massive lone pine tree, richly scented.

Grant broke the silence as he yelled to the Scouts and leaders below, waving and pointing to Mike. Mike felt embarrassed. He didn't want to attract attention, but Grant was proud of him, and Mike understood. He joined the waving. Those below stared at them. Mike knew what they were thinking. Who was this crazy guy hopping all over the mountains? Mike decided it was a good start. After all, he had a message to give them. That's why he was here instead of in Holland getting psyched up for the 100-meter dash.

Later that evening, a trip was made to Camp Wenton, a Boy Scout camp located on the shore of a large reservoir to the east of Mike's camp. A half-hour walk in the moonlit night brought the group to a barge, which took them across the water to camp. The camp was alive with dancing bonfires and groups of Scouts in various activities. Mike's group was greeted with warmth and vigor and brought right into the activities. Finally, Mike made his way over to the council fire for the program. He sat in silence, staring up at the massive rock to his left, then gazing westward past the camp and out over the lake. The full moon duplicated itself in the inky water and the waves shimmered it outward. Mike's eyes lifted to the dark shadows of the pines and on up into a sky twinkling with stars. Mike felt an intensely spiritual emotion sweep over him. He was awed by the beauty of it all and by the majesty of creation. He had always loved nature, but he had never felt such profound reverence before.

A Different Treasure   169

LDS Boy Scout Sesquicentennial Encampment in Eldorado National Forest
(courtesy of the *Placerville Mountain Democrat*)

The silence was broken by Scouts filing into the camp. Finally some three-hundred Scouts and leaders crammed the area, and the skits began. One after another, they were hilarious, crazy, corny. Campfire songs filled the cracks. The evening ended with a touching dismissal by one of the camp leaders, and the group filed out silently, as is the tradition with good campfires. Mike crawled into his sleeping bag very late that night. He felt chilly on the outside but very warm and contented on the inside. His decision to come seemed good.

The next day was mayhem. Parents were bringing the main group of Scouts up. Cars and confusion were everywhere. People were actually directing traffic under the green trees. Grant moved into a tent with his father and Gary Sargent moved into Mike's tent. Gary had also been a marine, a major. Now he was a lawyer in Salt Lake City and worked closely with the General Authorities of the Church. Mike would share the spotlight with this solid, quiet man. A late-morning flag ceremony found them at military attention. The Scouts were walking four abreast and lining up on the road in front of the teepee, facing the flagpole. When all were assembled, the national anthem began and the United States and California flags were slowly raised to the top of the pole. The two flags rippled against the sunny blue sky as the large crowd boomed out the Pledge of Allegiance. During the prayer Mike's emotions, sensitive and at the surface, overflowed. He relished the feeling of companionship and the surge of patriotism he felt for the flag. He felt no shame for the tears that blurred his vision.

After lunch Mike was wheeling around, surveying the camps set up by the troops, when a young Scout came stumbling breathlessly up to Mike.

"Mr. Johnson, there's a man down in our camp who would like to see you. He said to tell you he was in boot camp with you."

Mike had seen no one from boot camp or Vietnam in thirteen years. As he drifted down the hill toward the camp, a man with dark hair and a moustache approached. His eyes filled with tears as he put his hand over Mike's. Mike spoke first.

"Staff Sergeant Hubbard."

The not-so-strange stranger replied, "Platoon 127."

It was Mike's turn. "Sergeant Johnson."

"Sergeant Sands."

They had been testing each other with names from the past only they could share. Mike had forgotten how close he had felt to Bob McKenzie at boot camp. They worked through memories, laughed, then grew sober. They talked about Vietnam, what had happened since. Bob had been through hell as a helicopter gunner, then as a black marketer running the PXs and base exchanges and officers' clubs. Shady deals and life-style had carried him away from his religious roots. Only lately had Bob been coming back. This reunion nourished them both.

The days were filled with meals and ceremonies and contests and demonstrations, pole-latching, pancake throws, first aid, compass, and pioneering classes. On Saturday afternoon during a lull in the activity, Jay approached Mike.

"Brother Johnson, some of the men would like to see you climb that hill again. Would you do it for us?"

Was it a dare? a set-up? It didn't matter. Within a few minutes, Mike and Grant were again scrambling up the rock. It was a set-up. The booming loudspeaker announced, "If you would like to see Brother Johnson showing us how to climb a mountain the hard way, just look halfway up the cliff."

A Different Treasure

Mike felt a thousand pairs of eyes upon him and couldn't help feeling like a show-off. He didn't like the feeling or the awed hero worship afterwards that made it hard to talk easily with the boys.

Right after supper Mike met with the adult leaders and their senior patrol leaders. All too soon the contests were over and the time was Mike's to give a major address to the leaders. Mike sucked in his breath, his mind going a mile a minute. He still didn't know for sure what to say. Then it came to him; use the method of Jesus Christ. Teach a parable. Use what they knew, what they were involved with.

Mike talked about the fire-building contest and how the prize was eventually won. He then spoke of the lives of the Scouts in their respective troops as the prize, with the job of the leaders as the matches and kindling. The leaders had the responsibility of setting these Scouts on fire. They needed to burn hot and smoke-free because the boys were important and valuable. They looked up to the senior patrol leaders with great respect. "The Scoutmaster also expects you senior patrol leaders to be good leaders and responsible and not have to be told everything to do.

"You leaders are in one of the very finest organizations in the world. You have a fantastic opportunity to affect many lives for good; in fact, you may never know how important you are in the lives of these young men. But you will probably get just one chance, one turn, and this is it. Make it count. God bless you."

The group was right with Mike, hanging on every word. At his conclusion they rose in unison, each man and boy applauding as hard as he could. Leaders at the front hugged him. Mike was teary-eyed, filled with humbleness. He felt a great wave of responsibility. These people were honest with their feelings, and they cared for and respected him. He couldn't let them down. He had to give them everything he had, maybe even more if he could find it.

Later that night, Mike was supposed to speak to the whole camp, over a thousand men and boys. He was nervous. He didn't know what he would say.

The young Scouts marched into the meeting site four abreast, flags flying. Mike shivered with excitement and emotion as he sat on the stand between Jay Gould and Gary

Sargent. All grew quiet. Then a loud gasp went out in unison. Mike followed the eyes of the throng up to the top of the cliff. A figure dressed as an Indian, torches in both hands, stood on top of the rocks. He held the torches, brought them together, then separated them. That was the signal to light the huge council fire.

A young Scout immediately threw a switch to light the fire. Nothing happened. He tried again and again. Nothing. A couple of Explorer Scouts, older boys, began striking matches, but the tinder wasn't fine enough. A fast-thinking Scout ran for a gallon of gasoline and doused the logs; another Scout struck a match before the leaders could stop him, and the logs exploded into a fiery pillar. The boy with the gas can, shocked at the sudden explosion, turned and leaped from the fire, gasoline sloshing on his pants. A flame licked out, igniting his pants and shirt. Everyone was screaming, running, and throwing dirt.

Someone knocked the boy down and smothered the flames with a blanket. He was unhurt, so the program eventually continued; but it was off to a shaky start. Finally, the old carefree mood came back with skits, stories, songs, games, and jokes. It lasted for hours. The night was getting very cold now, and it was late. Jay edged toward Mike.

"Mike, it's so cold and late. Would you mind speaking tomorrow?"

Mike felt a burden lift. "Ah shucks, I was really planning on this, Brother Gould." He flashed Jay an impish look. But his relief didn't last long, and he barely slept.

Sunday dawned sunny and warm. It was a beautiful day. He watched the sun burst over the cliff as he faced it, sitting on the makeshift stand. Mike looked about him at the other leaders on the stand, then glanced down at his watch. It was 6:45 A.M., awfully early to start a Sunday morning, but the dawn was beautiful. Mike watched the boys file up and quietly take their place on the ground. Finally all was ready. At that moment Brother Casey, an older man who had been a Scouter for many years, quietly approached Mike.

"Brother Johnson, I would deem it a great honor to have you wear my Scout jacket up here on the stand." Mike examined the red jacket with important Scouting badges sewn neatly in place. He wanted to say, "No thanks," but then he realized the significance of the offer.

"Thank you, Brother Casey, I'd be glad to, if you're sure."

With that Mike took the red coat and handed the old man his Levi jacket. The old man wrung Mike's hand, his eyes full of love. It brought all Mike's emotions to the surface. Then the music from a thousand voices rising and echoing off the rocks of the mountain stirred Mike's soul.

Jay Gould stood at the microphone. "Brothers, you watched Brother Johnson climb to the top of that peak up there. Brother Johnson's life has been like that mountain of rock, boulders looming up, like his tragic war injuries. We saw his fighting spirit as he clawed his way up that mountain. That's exactly what Michael Johnson has done in life—climbed his way up past huge obstacles to reach a great peak of success. Brother Johnson is a great example to all of us."

Mike knew what they'd all tell their folks when they got home. He felt a little embarrassed, but then he thought that most of those boys had probably never known anyone in a wheelchair. They probably thought you were somehow bolted in. He almost chuckled. It probably did freak them out to see someone frog-hop to the top of that mountain.

Grant shoved him up to the front of the stage. Mike stuck a rock behind each wheel and began. He told the boys about Vietnam and how he ended up in the chair. He told them about the ramp in Philadelphia and how important it was in his recovery. Mike talked about ramps they would face in their lives.

"Working your way to the top of your personal ramps will create strength and character in you. Use that strength to become Eagle Scouts and successful missionaries. Don't let the little things in life get in the way of fulfilling your commitments."

The crowd rose almost at once, applauding thunderously. Mike waved and nodded, then tried to push back from center stage, but something held him. It was Jay Gould.

"Brother Johnson, we'd like to hear a bit about how you met your wife and about your family. Go on and tell us about that."

Mike liked this subject. He talked about his romance with Jan, their marriage, their children. Once again Mike closed and began to back away. Once again the applause filled the natural arena, echoing up and over the hills.

Jay Gould stood at the microphone again. "Men, I want to tell you something very special about Brother Johnson, something I just figured out in the past few days. Most of you prob-

Receiving commemorative buffalo skull
(courtesy of the *Placerville Mountain Democrat*)

ably don't know that Mike is an outstanding wheelchair athlete. He was a champion in the 1976 Olympics. Brother Johnson was invited to the 1980 Olympics in Holland. They were held this same week that we have been here. Mike missed the Olympics so he could be here with you, sharing his great strength."

Jay's voice broke as he forced out the final sentences. He wiped his eyes with a handkerchief. The crowd was silent.

"Mike, we'd like to hear about your athletics. Could you tell us about wheelchair basketball and track and field and the 1976 Olympics?"

Mike started at the beginning. He talked about playing basketball in a wheelchair, explained the intricacies of wheelchair track and field, described the slalom. They were all right there in the chair with Mike, wheeling through the barriers, backing up, shooting over the narrow trestles of the bridge, streaking for the finish line.

A Different Treasure 175

Then Mike told them about the 1976 Olympics. He told them about the bald Egyptian and the ricocheting ping-pong balls. They roared with laughter, sparked by Mike's infectious grin. When he started talking about the blind racers, he had to swallow hard against the lump growing in his throat.

"Brothers, I had a fantastic time, but it was much more than that. I went to Toronto thinking I was going to whip the world. Mike Johnson, king of track and field. Then, at the Olympics, I saw men and women much more dedicated than myself, with disabilities so much worse than mine."

Mike paused, concentrated on steadying his voice. He thought of that black, bleak year of despair and his voice wavered again. "I wouldn't have Jan or Seth or Matthew or Rachel if I hadn't gone through that experience. I probably wouldn't be here speaking to you today. I'm not sure I would have worked with kids if I hadn't had my injuries. So you can see that the things I value the most in life, everything that is most precious to me, has come after the land mine and in many ways because of it. We all have land mines in our lives. Let's all work together to help each other make great success out of our tragedies." He whispered, "I love you all very much. Thank you for sharing your lives and time with me."

Mike paused, then added very emphatically, "This time I really am through."

The standing ovation went on and on. Jay Gould hugged Mike for a long time, his tears falling on the collar of Mike's shirt.

The next morning Mike was staring through the window of the jet heading east to Utah. He thought of the night before, of the boys who had asked for his autograph, taken pictures with him. He thought of the aged Hawaiian who had given him a beautifully carved eagle neckerchief clasp. He smiled at the thought of the big buffalo skull he had received: "Sesquicentennial Encampment—Pedler Hill, July 1980, Mike Johnson" burned across the forehead. There was the little Scout who had proudly pushed Mike's wheelchair up the incline to his tent so Mike could put the skull where it would be safe.

The camp had easily been worth Holland, Mike thought. He could have gone for the gold, but now he wanted a different treasure.

Mike wheeled off the tarmac and through the door of the

airport. There were Jan and the kids. Seth and Matt broke away from Jan yelling, "Daddy, Daddy." Little Rachel struggled in vain to get out of the stroller. The boys swarmed over Mike's chair. They wheeled over to Jan and Rachel. Rachel was in the chair now, too. Mike looked up at Jan's smiling eyes.

"Welcome home."

14

Home

Donald Shaw, assistant dean of the BYU College of Physical Education, leaned back in his office chair and studied the wood paneling on the wall. Clayne Jensen, the dean of the BYU College of Physical Education had been in.

Don had told him about Mike Johnson. He'd be graduating in health science in April but wouldn't be able to attend the ceremony because he was involved in a Wood Badge training program at Maple Dell Scout Camp.

The dean had been surprised. "That's a pretty rigid, elite training program for Scout leaders, isn't it? How could a guy in a wheelchair successfully participate in that type of program?"

Don was anxious to answer. "Well, this kid's unique. He's a hunter, fisherman, athlete. I don't think his lack of legs stops him from doing very much at all. Clayne, Wood Badge is one of the highest awards for Scouters in the leadership phase of Scouting. Just to be invited is a real honor reserved for outstanding leaders. I'd like to honor Mike by presenting him with his certificate of graduation up at Maple Dell. Would it be possible?"

The dean looked at his colleague. "Let's work it out, Don."

Mike knew that Jan, her parents, and the kids were coming to the final ceremonies. But he wondered why Don Shaw was there. Mike couldn't wait to tell Jan about the ten days he had just spent. He had scaled a tower lashed together with poles,

Attending Wood Badge training program at Maple Dell Scout Camp, April 1980

Jan proudly watches as Mike receives certificate of graduation from BYU, presented by Donald Shaw, Assistant Dean

pulling himself up by his hands, the muscles in his arms and shoulders giving every ounce of strength they had. Each day he had pulled himself over rough terrain and obstacles. He had been elected patrol leader. He had loved the program.

At the conclusion of the awards ceremony, Dr. Shaw was invited to march to the center of the circle. Then a surprised Mike Johnson was escorted by his patrol up to the awards stand. Wood Badge and graduation in one day! Mike turned a half-circle in his chair to face his family. Jan had tears streaming down her face. Jan's mom was holding her tight. Walt Cryer's smiling lips spelled out a mute "congratulations." With a large knot in his throat, Mike opened his arms to his children, who were dashing across the parade ground, then engulfing him. Emotion swept through the ranks of Scouters. It was an experience they would tearfully relate to their own families. A thunderous ovation filled the field.

That ovation was still in his ears as he lay in his sleeping bag. He could hear the heavy breathing of his sleeping sons. They were camped in the hills just north of Alpine. He was thinking about Scout camp too.

His mind drifted back to Vietnam. Mike's dad had been a marine in World War II. Those soldiers had been welcomed home as conquering heroes in an American embrace. It hadn't been like that for Mike's friends. People hated the war, wanted to forget. But those who had been in those jungles had a harder time forgetting.

"Most of us didn't know why we were there," Mike thought, looking up at the stars. "We were just fighting to survive a year of confusion. Our South Vietnamese allies were mired in corruption. The military tactics seemed futile—take it by day, lose it by night. Then call the choppers to take out the mutilated."

Mike had been among that group. Part of the body count. That was how they measured success or failure in that war. He gritted his teeth. The Veterans Administration had labeled him 100 percent disabled, total and permanent. He was supposed to be a package sitting quietly on a shelf somewhere, opening his mouth to be fed. He wasn't going to live down to those expectations. The normal feelings and desires, the competitive spirit that he had grown up with, were still there in that maimed body.

He thought of his body with pride now. For a long time he had been angry at it, resentful of it, ashamed and embarrassed. But it had climbed his mountains, won his races, loved his wife, fathered his children, and served his church. He let out his breath quietly. There were lots of things he could have done differently with a whole body, but he wasn't sure that he could have done them better. He savored that pride and self-respect. It had been a long time coming.

Mike thought of the fighting. The roar reminded him of summer thunderstorms, only loud, murderous, brief, usually pointless. That wasn't what killed in Vietnam. What killed was insidious, quick, and frustratingly quiet—booby traps, pungi sticks, trip wires. No wonder there was such a huge problem with grass, speed, heroin, opium.

Why had Mike been spared? How had he come through? He thought of Jan and knew the answer. He had people who cared. Jan and the kids kept life in perspective. Being a husband and father kept Mike from drowning in self-pity. Mike had them to care about. He had his Scouts.

And he had his faith. He knew God, and he knew Mike Johnson was a son of God. This life prepared for the next life. Mike would have his legs back again. He wasn't holding his breath, but it was still a great thought.

That night under the stars, with his two little boys unconscious of what was going on, Mike Johnson knew that he could handle what life had for him. He was almost all the way home.

On 20 August 1980, Joseph joined the Johnson family. When Eli arrived on 20 February 1982, Mike made a big decision.

In a six-month period his use of sleeping medications had gotten progressively worse; he was using more and more and waking up later and later. One early afternoon Mike awoke in his normal confused and fuzzy state. "Wow, I've got to get off this stuff before I lose everything."

Mike rolled out of bed and hopped to the phone, then shakily dialed the VA Hospital.

"Dr. Romney, I need to get off some heavy drugs I'm taking for sleep, along with some pain medication. I've tried . . ." Mike's voice cracked as he choked up. "I've tried to do it myself several times, sir, but it's too strong. I've gotta have some help."

Dr. Romney's voice was strong and steady. It reminded Mike of his grandfather's. "Mike, I'm convinced we can help you. Can you tell me what you're on and how much?"

"Yes, sir, I'm taking two or three Seconal a night with a few

Mepergan Fortis, and sometimes some Quaaludes." After a brief pause Mike continued, "That's a lot, isn't it? But I'm so scared of night coming. All I think about in the day is how I'm going to get to sleep at night."

The doctor didn't respond to Mike's question. "Mike I want you to come directly to Salt Lake City right now and check into the VA Hospital. Don't eat breakfast or anything. There are two wards you can go in. I'll put you in the best one for you. We will expect you in an hour."

Mike silently packed a bag, tearfully told Jan what was happening, and then reached for her. Their embrace was one of insecurity, each holding tightly for fear of losing the other. Jan finally gained control and was the first to speak.

"Michael, I love you so deeply. Seeing you go downhill these past months . . ." She hesitated while Mike tenderly wiped tears off her cheek. How many times during distant noons had she emotionally blurted out, "Michael, you've got to stop taking those drugs. You aren't yourself. I don't like it. It's going to destroy you." The distance had increased between them. They had survived too much to have this happen. "Oh, Mike, you have so much potential, you have so much to offer other people, young people, your own kids." Jan choked back a few sobs, then continued.

"I know I've been miserable to live with, but when I'm up with the kids and you're lying in bed in a drugged sleep . . ."

"Oh, Janny, you're a wonderful lady. I don't know how you've hung in there this long. I'm gonna make it this time. You deserve more, so much more."

An hour later a very scared Mike rolled through the doors of the VA Hospital, not quite aware that two weeks of hell were waiting.

Faced with what Mike thought was typical VA efficiency, he waited and waited in the reception room. He pored through magazines, not really seeing them, continually wiping sweat from his face. As the minutes ticked by, Mike's apprehension and nervousness grew. He felt ready to blow, yet fought the incessant urge to leave and finally parked himself against the wall, locked the brakes, and tried to get lost in a Louis L'Amour western. A psychiatrist finally discovered him.

"Gosh, Mike, I'm very sorry. Dr. Romney told me you were coming right up. I thought the receptionist would bring you right in."

The interview was straightforward, an information session

about the amount and type of drugs taken, not why. Maybe the psychiatrist thought he knew. When the doctor was called out for a moment Mike glanced at his notes. They read, "Patient extremely apprehensive, potentially suicidal."

"Where did he ever get an idea like that?" Mike was now very confused and shaking with nervousness. Maybe the situation was more desperate than he had realized.

A psychology intern who would prove to be a real asset to Mike was assigned to him and took Mike to the ward. The click of the lock in the door behind Mike gave him an eerie feeling, but the ultimate insult was the yell and laugh from an inmate, Curtis Strange.

"Hey, Johnson, what are you, the all-American college man, doing in here—studying psychology?" A loud, rude laugh followed. Mike had been a psychology aide supervising Curtis at the Utah State Mental Hospital; now he was a patient with Curtis. The reality of his situation smacked Mike, and he reeled with the psychological blow.

After the initial reaction Curtis settled down and showed genuine interest in Mike. "What are you in here for, Johnson? I know you're not nuts." The psychology intern jumped into the conversation.

"Mike has been on sleep meds a long time. He has come in here to get off them." It was clear, simple, and easy.

"Oh well, good luck, Mike. If I can help you in any way, let me know." With that, Curtis was gone. The program was underway.

The sights, sounds, smells, patients, and VA personnel were all too familiar to Mike—an uneasy, deathlike familiarity. The smoky, dank, dead air with a faint unpleasant odor; tuberculosis and lung-cancer coughing of old men; old rotten buildings and half-dead people, apathy—all of it rang distant bells and pricked familiar emotions in Mike. He didn't like it, didn't like this part of his past, and felt trapped. It was a cold, sweaty feeling and made him want to bust out, get in the Jimmy and drive. The desert! What he needed was the desert and solitude. But the desert hadn't helped him overcome his drug problem, not with all its beauty and serenity and peacefulness. "How could this rotten, stinking place help me?"

"Hey man, what you in here for?" Mike jerked about and stared into a heavily bearded face framed by long straight hair. Intense blue eyes showed age and rage and confusion and in-

Riding on Veterans float in a Provo Fourth of July parade

quisitiveness. The bottom lip opened to say something else, then hesitated. A slight movement to the right of the hair—Mike noticed a tall black whose face was mellow and easy.

"Hi guys. Ah—I'm Mike Johnson. I'm in here to get off some sleep meds I've been on since 'Nam."

The word " 'Nam" caused the chemistry. Mike became the confidant, his two new friends his protectors. They were both Vietnam vets who had never fully returned and probably never would. Ron, the giant bearded one, lived in Vietnam. That was all he could relate to. Ron reminded Mike of a human Mount St. Helens, rumbling and smoking, ready to blow sky high. Lester, the black vet, was mellow and a follower. Anything Ron did or thought was okay with him. Both vets intuitively realized Mike's head was on pretty straight and for hours pulled from him anything that would make sense in their crazy, confused worlds. Mike was good for them, but the relationship was not symbiotic. He didn't need to relive 'Nam. The world he was presently in was much more important.

The first three days were very difficult for Mike because it was the weekend and no doctors were around. Mike was admitted to the hospital Friday at noon. All drugs were given up then. By late Friday afternoon he was becoming very antsy about the approaching night. He spotted a nurse at the desk.

"Ma'am, uh, this is my first night here. I'm being detoxified, but I'm in pain and I can't just quit cold turkey. When can I have something to get me to sleep?"

The vacant look which swept the nurse's face told Mike he was in trouble! All doctors had left for the weekend at 4:00 P.M. No record of Mike's program or any orders for him had been left at the nurse's station.

"This is so typical VA," Mike muttered under his breath, then firmly convinced the nurse to phone a doctor. Shots of Demerol kept Mike sane until a doctor visited him and set up a withdrawal program Sunday evening. He was on his way. His medicine, a combination of methadone and Valium, was taken morning, noon, and evening. Doses were gradually cut down. Nights were the worst. Mike lay there staring at the ceiling, trying to settle his head down, but responding nervously to the hospital night sounds.

Each morning through the long two weeks, group-therapy sessions were held. One therapist and twelve to fourteen patients made up the group. Mike hated the group sessions; they seemed so useless to him, even damaging. He described his impressions of the sessions in a letter to Jan.

"Janny, these group therapy sessions are *crazy*. First a therapist, usually a student, tells us right from a psychology book 'This is the stage you are in now.' Then we hear more hocus-pocus about colors and cognitive triangles and junk that nobody in the group understands. Then the people tear into each other, they start tearing someone down. Yesterday they tore apart this real heavy, homely girl who was in the service and has tried to kill herself many times. She had a baby some time ago and it was taken away. Anyway she is a born loser, doesn't think anyone in the world cares about her. This group climbed her frame, called her stupid, 'you can't really think that,' just tore her apart.

"I couldn't handle it, Jan. I butted in, tried to defend her, and got threatened. Ron the mountain man and Lester jumped in and defended me. Nobody plays around with Ron! It's like they're my personal bodyguards. Anyhow, the therapists do nothing, just sit there and even help the crucifixion, then they go into a staff meeting. Meanwhile this poor girl's crying hysterically. Nobody even tries to put her back together. I'm glad they've never gotten to me.

"I'm thinking the staff shouldn't even be in these meetings, they're useless. We should talk these things out ourselves, have a real meeting. They just talk about what they are doing, never why. No one gets a chance to tell what they need, to talk about something that relates to them—right from the book, 'this is the stage you are in now!' Who the flip cares! I want to know why I am taking all these drugs. They never get into that. I find myself thinking 'Why am I sitting here listening to these students practicing and not helping these people who have major head troubles?' There has got to be a better way, Janny, to help these poor people.

"Sure do miss you and the kids, Jan. See you Monday."

Monday finally arrived and Mike excitedly headed for the shower. He hadn't seen his family in over a week, and a few hours at Hogle Zoo with them would be a real treat. "I love my family." Though he felt jittery and on edge from the continual decrease of medication, Mike felt sure he could handle it. Someone was in the adjoining shower. Mike slid his towel over to make room for his own. Suddenly a deep, angry voice boomed out, "Take your hands off my towel. I'm going to break your face." Startled, Mike jerked around in time to see a huge body fill the shower entrance. It was the ex-marine everyone had told him about, a massive strong man whose greatest desire was to hurt people, anybody, for anything! He had been kicked out of other mental institutions because of his viciousness. Mike had avoided him, until now.

There he was, a massive hulking Goliath with murder in his eyes. Mike instinctively tugged at his armrest and held it up defensively. Mike's mind was moving faster than his heart was pounding. "He's coming out of the shower after me, right now. Here we go. What do I do, scream for help?"

"I'm gonna kill you tonight. Enjoy today, man, it's your last." An ugly scowl finished Goliath's threat, and back into the shower he went. Mike headed for the director's office.

"Sir, I just can't handle what's going on around here. I'm not a complainer, but I came here to get help. Now I've got these crazy Vietnam vets dragging my head back to all the ugliness of 'Nam, and King Kong threatens me with death. I don't need to go back to 'Nam a whole bunch of times. It isn't good for my head to review 'Nam and all the things I've seen. I can't take this idiot threatening me. I just want to get off these drugs!" Mike never saw Goliath again, and his two friends softened their Vietnam discussions.

The zoo and being with his family were therapy for Mike. He could sense Jan's pride in him. She knew it was extremely difficult, but hoped it would make a very positive impact on their family. "It's worth it, Mike. Just one more week. You can make it, Hon'." Mike could see the longing in Jan's eyes for the real Michael Johnson she had married to come back to her, the Mike Johnson who was not strung out and controlled by chemicals. He would, somehow he would. The lowering levels of medication in Mike's body heightened his nervousness. Every movement, every noise found Mike's eyes darting toward it. Everything seemed so intensified and accelerated. After almost leaping out of his chair when one of the kids yelled, Mike looked up at Jan, who was covering her mouth with her hand.

"Sorry, Janny, I'm strung tighter than a piano wire."

The afternoon was very emotional for Mike. Too soon it was a teary "so long" for kids who couldn't understand why Dad couldn't come home with them. Mike lay awake long into the night knowing he had to succeed. He just couldn't fail this time. It was too important, affected too many lives.

Life went on, the drugs were continuously cut down, and Mike's brother Steve actively helped him through the second week.

"I'm gonna try to help you all I can. I'll come up anytime you need me. Just let me know, Mike." He called Steve several times.

Friday finally arrived, with lower drug levels in Mike's body than he had known since leaving Vietnam. Mike's two "buddies," Lester and Ron, were close to tears at seeing Mike go. He had become their one sane friend in a crazy world. Mike couldn't leave without doing something for Sue, "the girl most likely to commit suicide."

"Guys, get that crazy secretary out of the office and I'll order some flowers."

The flowers arrived while Sue was doing crafts, but almost weren't delivered to her.

"I'm sorry, Mr. Johnson," the ancient nurse smacked together her purple-red lips, her eyes and face forceful. "I'm in charge here, Buster. We can't just give Sue these flowers. She may not be allowed to have flowers on her program. I'll have to check with the psychiatrist!"

She walked away in a military manner and telephoned. Mike watched her every movement and at an opportune time grabbed the flowers. He quickly wheeled into Sue's room, where he found the right spot to place the beautiful bouquet.

It was half an hour before Sue came back to the ward, a sad look on her face.

"Hi, Sue."

"Hi, guys." The door to her room closed quietly. The three looked at each other and smiled. Meeting someone else's needs had a warm magic in it. Then they watched the door.

It finally opened, quietly and slowly. Tears were streaming down Sue's face.

"Oh, you guys." She was too choked up to say more. She didn't have to; she just bawled like a baby. Mike and his two friends understood. No one had ever done anything nice for her before, showed her they cared or liked her. Finally someone was saying, "We care, you are a human being." Even Nurse "Follow-the-Book" had tears well up in her eyes. The discovery of caring is a magical moment.

Mike decided to stay for lunch before he left. It was a major mistake! An old man Mike had become very fond of clutched his chest, forced out a tight groan, and collapsed on the floor. He began to turn blue as confusion swept around him. Finally, as Mike, horrified, watched the blue turn darker and inky, a physician arrived. He began CPR, but Mike knew he was too late. It was a depressing send-off.

During the ride home Mike could think of only one thing. The hospital hadn't sent home any medication and there was none at home. This was it! He thought of what he knew about methadone, a heroin substitute of which Ron had said, "It ain't easy to come off, Johnson. You go a little wacko for a while." Little knowing it, Ron was prophesying about the next four days in the life of Mike Johnson.

That night Mike lay in bed thrashing and moaning, trying desperately to escape from whatever was eating him up inside. The VA had said, "Okay, Johnson, you're done, you're okay now. Go home and enjoy your family." "Here I am Jan. I'm all better."

But he wasn't. In fact, coming off the methadone made Mike feel he was losing his mind, going crazy as he never believed he could be. Finally Mike rolled off the bed and hopped to the shower, desperately seeking any kind of comfort. He turned on the water and moved into the stream. A thousand hot needles were suddenly driven through him again and again. His whole body felt on fire. Mike crawled back on the bed and moaned and cried and thrashed into the night. He prayed as he thrashed about: "Oh God, Heavenly Father, I would just as soon be dead. Why do I have to go through this too? Haven't I had enough? Oh, please give me a break. I've just gotta have some help."

For four days the black nightmare hovered over and drove through him—Mike's eyes were never closed in sleep, not in four days and three nights. He didn't dare come out of his bedroom or let the kids in for fear of what he might do or say. Mike didn't want his kids to hear him pray to die, then shout and scream and roll like a crazy man.

Then, in a lucid moment, Mike heard sobbing and recognized it wasn't his. He cleared his mind as best he could and located the muffled noise—it was coming from the chute to the basement laundry room. He listened carefully. In between the sobs were sentences:

"There's just no way I can take this. I have no training. Mike is just crazy. Here I am, pregnant. What do I do?" More sobs and crying took over the words.

Mike thought of Jan holding him like a son with a high fever, pulling him close to her and rocking, softly talking as she tried to control her own emotions. Jan had called Steve, called the bishop, asking for special blessings to unwind Mike. She was a beautiful woman, and as soon as this torment passed Mike resolved to love his wife the way she deserved to be loved.

Late afternoon of the fourth day found Mike lying exhausted on the living room floor, staring with eyes fused open at a familiar ceiling. Jan's mother had just walked in the front door.

"Mike, how are you feeling? Are you sleeping better?"

Mike gave his mother-in-law a perplexed stare:

"Mom, I haven't slept one minute, not one wink, in four days."

"Oh, Mike." Mrs. Cryer's brow wrinkled. "That's impossible, you have slept some, you just don't remember it."

Jan quickly entered into the conversation.

Teaching science at American Fork Junior High School

Coaching girls basketball team at American Fork Junior High School

Michael and Jan Johnson with their family, 1985 —
Seth, 8 (top left); Matt, 7; Joe, 5; David, 2; Eli, 3; Rachel, 6

"Mom, honest, Mike hasn't closed his eyes in four days. He hasn't slept." Tears welled up in Jan's eyes. "It's really been horrible."

"Well, it's got to happen soon. We're all praying for you."

That night Mike finally slept, fitfully at first, then later dropping into a deeper, more peaceful sleep. In the days that followed he slowly unwound, and Jan joyfully welcomed *her* Michael back.

It was a nightmare, but Mike and Jan had fought and won. It was another mountain to climb, another race to win. But this time he didn't need the applauding crowds at the end to keep him going. That clean taste of self-respect was enough.

Now, in the winter of 1985, Mike still feels that sense of home. David is two years old. Mike serves as a Primary teacher in his LDS ward. Jan is the ward Primary inservice leader and is expecting baby number seven in the spring (so much for the garden!). Mike teaches science and coaches the girls' basketball team at American Fork Junior High. He still loves athletics and turns on to competition, but somehow he doesn't need to win to prove anything.

Mike knows he is home—all the way home.